British Subministers
and Colonial America

British Subministers
and Colonial America
1763-1783

by Franklin B. Wickwire

PRINCETON, NEW JERSEY
PRINCETON UNIVERSITY PRESS
1966

Copyright © 1966 by Princeton University Press
All Rights Reserved
Library of Congress Catalog Card Number: 66-10274

Publication of this book has been aided by
the Whitney Darrow Publication Reserve Fund
of Princeton University Press.

Printed in the United States of America
by Princeton University Press, Princeton, New Jersey

For Bob and Lewis

PREFACE

THE following work attempts to analyze the importance of secretaries and undersecretaries in five important British administrative departments to the determination of British colonial policy during the period of the American Revolution. It focuses upon the most important measures that led to the Revolution and illumines the role of the subministers in either proposing or implementing those measures.

In order to achieve this purpose the work necessarily divides itself into two parts, one dealing with the organization of the departments in which the minor men worked and the second with their work during the revolutionary period. The first part, therefore, describes the differences and similarities between the secretaries to the admiralty, board of trade, treasury, customs, and the undersecretaries of state; the nature of the departments they served; and their work within those departments. The second part shows their influence on the measures that led to the American Revolution and their work in prosecuting the war itself.

I am indebted to many people for making possible this study. Perhaps my first thanks should go to Professor Robert R. Rea, who interested me in the subject in my first graduate seminar and has encouraged me in it ever since. I owe much to Professor Lewis P. Curtis, who maintained my interest in the project and corrected my many errors when guiding me through my Ph.D. dissertation. Mr. Bernhard Knollenberg suggested some areas of investigation which I might otherwise have overlooked. My acknowledgments must also go to Professor Edward Greaves, to Mr. Ian Christie, to the late Pro-

fessor Mark Thomson, and to the late Sir Lewis Namier
for their valuable aid, advice, suggestions, and encouragement.

I owe a great debt to Mr. W. S. Lewis for permitting
me to examine his microfilm collection of Newcastle
papers, and to Mr. George Lam for his time and trouble
in steering me through that valuable source. Sir John
Murray kindly allowed me to examine his collection
of Grenville papers in London, a very important collection for the letters of Treasury Secretary Whately. Although I found little pertinent to my study in those portions of the Sandwich papers that have not been published, Mr. Victor Montagu's interest in my topic and
his allowing me to examine the Sandwich papers at Mapperton Manor in Dorset typified the unfailing courtesy
afforded me in Britain.

Thanks are due the staff of the Sterling Memorial
Library for their help and cooperation. The trustees of
the British Museum and the officials of the Public Record
Office kindly permitted me to use the many manuscripts
so necessary for my study. The Lincoln Record Office and
the William Salt Library at Stafford allowed me to examine collections pertinent to my work. The unfailing courtesy and cooperation of the staff of the William L. Clements Library, and especially Mr. W. E. Ewing and the
director Mr. Howard Peckham, made my work at Ann
Arbor both fruitful and enjoyable.

A Samuel Fels fellowship generously allowed me the
necessary funds to pursue research in America and England, and a grant from the research council of the University of Massachusetts provided the funds so necessary
for typing, traveling, purchasing of supplies, and all the

Preface

other details that sometimes seem to overshadow, at least in their strain of the nerves, research and writing.

Lastly, thanks must go to my wife, without whose advice and encouragement I could never have completed this work.

CONTENTS

xi

Contents

British Subministers
and Colonial America

ABBREVIATIONS

The following abbreviations are used:

H.M.C.	Historical Manuscripts Commission
P.R.O.	Public Record Office
B.M.	British Museum
MSS Add.	Additional Manuscripts
D.N.B.	*Dictionary of National Biography*
O.S.	Old Style—dates according to the Julian Calendar, in use in England before 1752.

All other works have been cited in full the first time and abbreviated every time they are cited thereafter. Any confusing abbreviations in quotations from eighteenth-century sources have been eliminated.

INTRODUCTION

The Subministers
and British Colonial Policy

MOST Victorian histories of eighteenth-century Britain focused on the major events and prominent politicians, statesmen, soldiers, sailors, ecclesiastics, artists, and men of letters. Although nineteenth-century historians were unprepared to search deeply into special areas such as economic history, administrative history, history of science, and so on, they had both the materials and the competence for describing much better than they did the importance of the secretaries and undersecretaries to government departments, to British politics, and to administration. Perhaps these secretaries and undersecretaries, or subministers, received less than deserved attention because of their relative unobtrusiveness and humble status when working or mixing socially with the great aristocrats. As Sir Lewis Namier—assuredly no Victorian—stated: "Both the dignity and inferiority of the chaplain or curate at a big country house attached to their persons and position—they had to know a great deal and not expect too much, to be qualified to sit at the table of their chief, and, in most cases, be satisfied with the lowest places at it."[1]

Their relatively inferior social status, however, belies their bureaucratic standing. Their chiefs may have seated them at the lowest places of the table, but they probably listened to the subministers far more than to their social equals when administration came under dis-

[1] Sir Lewis Namier, *The Structure of Politics at the Accession of George III*, 2d ed. (London, 1957), p. 37.

3

cussion. Indeed, that the subministerial voice rang with authority in administrative decisions has been increasingly recognized by twentieth-century historians. As early as 1912 Mary P. Clarke pointed out the influence of the secretary to the board of trade. She suggested his importance to nearly all phases of the board's activities. In 1917 William T. Laprade published the parliamentary papers of John Robinson, revealing his vital labors as treasury secretary in the general election of 1784. Since Laprade's publication, several works have touched upon Robinson's performance as Lord North's treasury secretary. Dora Mae Clark demonstrated the importance, in formulating treasury policy, not only of Robinson, but of the treasury secretaries in general. Sir Lewis Namier cited some of the occasions when Admiralty Secretary John Cleveland influenced administrative and political decisions. Recently Jack Sosin illustrated the important role that Undersecretary of State William Knox played in the Quebec Act. Kenneth Ellis devoted a considerable portion of his study of the English post office in the eighteenth century to one of its secretaries, Anthony Todd, acknowledged by his contemporaries to be the most important and influential man in the department.[2] Thus scholars have begun to lift the subministers from obscurity into prominence as useful parts of eighteenth-century government machinery.

[2] See William T. Laprade, "Public Opinion and the General Election of 1784," *English Historical Review*, xxxi (1916), 224-237, and Laprade, ed., *The Parliamentary Papers of John Robinson, 1774-1784* (Camden Society Publications, third series, xxxiii [London, 1922]); Dora Mae Clark, "The Office of Secretary to the Treasury in the Eighteenth Century," *American Historical Review*, xlii (1936-1937), 22-45, and *The Rise of the British Treasury* (New Haven, 1960), *passim*; Namier, *Structure*, pp. 39-43; Jack M. Sosin, *Whitehall and the Wilderness* (Lincoln, Neb., 1961), pp. 239-249; and Kenneth Ellis, *The Post Office in the Eighteenth Century* (London, 1958), esp. the second half of the work.

4

Subministers & British Colonial Policy

Competent administrators, of course, are not only useful but necessary to any organizational machinery. Tudor government found indispensable the services of its Cromwells, Walsinghams, and Cecils, as did Stuart government those of its Cecils, Nicholases, and Hydes. Britain's great reforms of the nineteenth century and its sprawling but competently governed empire owed much to the Chadwicks, Trevelyans, and Stephenses. They always, seemingly, unraveled the increasing complexities of a growing, industrialized world power.

The eighteenth century, perhaps even more than those centuries which preceded or followed it, needed competent subministers. The leading Tudor and Stuart ministers were also prominent, and often highly competent, administrators. It could be feasibly argued that when their political ambitions exceeded their administrative competence government tended to break down. The nineteenth century separated administrators from politicians. Administrators, i.e., the civil servants, had security of tenure in government positions designed, apparently, to carry out decisions made by the cabinet members—politicians who trooped constantly in and out of power. Disraeli and the conservatives might acquire empire and lose political office. Gladstone and the liberals might lose empire and gain political office. The civil servants retained administrative office permanently and helped, supposedly with impartiality, whichever politician happened to form a ministry to give away or acquire territory. The eighteenth century made no such fine distinctions. The most important politicians were still supposed to be competent administrators like their Stuart predecessors. Yet the game of politics in the Hanoverian era allowed the politicians little time to acquire administrative competence. The earlier Tudor or Stuart ministers, once

5

secure in the monarch's favor, could devote their energies to administration. The Hanoverian politicians needed the monarch's and Parliament's favor to stay in power. If they secured neither they looked to future office by cultivating the heir apparent or seeking fame "out-of-doors." In any event, pursuing office or holding it demanded relentless attention to matters of patronage, electioneering, factional maneuvering, and parliamentary tactics.

During the reign of George III these pursuits required even more attention than earlier in the century. Seeking of followers, political alliances and betrayals, factional maneuvering, and vituperation in pamphlet war reached a pitch probably not seen since the days of Queen Anne. Politicians hungrily seeking office had little time to study administration, nor had they time, once in office, to learn it by experience. Ministerial tenures were remarkably short between 1760 and 1770. Even during Lord North's comparatively long and stable government, 1770-1782, there were three different secretaries to the American department between 1770 and 1775. This department had become the most important governmental office in the determination of colonial policy by 1770, yet its heads changed nearly every two years from that date to the outbreak of hostilities on Lexington Green. By the time North, as first lord of the treasury, had acquired peacetime administrative experience, and by the time the North government had settled down, ministers faced a new set of difficulties, the outbreak of rebellion in America, followed by war with France. Under such circumstances few of George III's leading ministers before the advent of the younger Pitt learned the fine details of administration.

Of necessity they left these details to the subministers —the secretaries, undersecretaries, and certain permanent board members such as the customs commissioners. If the first lord of the treasury, for example, contemplated a revision of customs procedure, he would assuredly consult, before all others, the customs commissioners and their secretary. Because of their experience the commissioners and the secretary would probably present more sensible advice than anyone else. The customs commissionerships may have been, as Namier noted, "a suitable retreat for Members who for some reason or other had, or wished to leave Parliament—from men broken in health or disappointed in their bolder hopes and ambitions,"[3] but for just that reason the commissioners were more likely to know their business than the "political" first lord or his politicking friends. The customs commissioners had more time to concentrate on it, because they had given up political ambitions. A secretary of state usually sought his undersecretary's advice on matters relative to the department rather than anyone else's. The undersecretary opened the mail, supervised the office, and knew the men of all ranks at the various embassies. His administrative suggestions obviously merited closer attention than those of many intimate friends of the secretary of state, even though the friends might have interests in the same county, belong to prominent families, or vote invariably with the secretary of state in Parliament. The very nature of the undersecretary's office, as well as other secretarial offices, guaranteed a thorough grounding in administration and, on that basis, an almost unimpeded influence in administrative matters.

Could the subministers' influence extend beyond administration to the making of policy? Administrative matters must of necessity sometimes dictate important

[3] Namier, *Structure*, p. 21.

governmental decisions. If, for example, the customs commissioners recommended to the first lord of the treasury enlarging the customs establishment, the first lord might take the momentous political step of appealing to Parliament for increased grants of money. Because they were the most important administrators, the subministers must thus sometimes have influenced the political decisions of their superiors on the basis of administrative necessity.

But if the exigencies of politics coupled with administration to thrust the subministers forward, a second factor—intimacy with the powerful—also propelled them into key roles. Even the most experienced politician-administrator will be prone to utilize fully subordinates whose years of administrative service equal or exceed his own. He will be especially prone to do so if he is a personal friend of the subordinate or has personal knowledge of a subordinate's ability (as opposed to knowledge of the subordinate's reputation for ability). The eighteenth-century politicians usually acquired such knowledge, for bureaucracy was far smaller, and in a sense more informal, than the vast impersonal machine of the civil service today. Professional "civil servants" such as the admiralty secretaries, staffed that bureaucracy, and private agents of the leading politicians assumed "civil service" positions in the bureaucracy, such as many of the undersecretaries of state and secretaries to the treasury.[4] If the dividing line was thin, these subministers all had one thing in common. They had previously enjoyed, or immediately acquired, a private intimacy with their superiors, for many of those superiors still believed, far

[4] A more detailed statement of the difference between the professionals and the politicians appears in Franklin B. Wickwire, "King's Friends, Civil Servants, or Politicians," *A.H.R.*, LXXI (1965), 18-42.

more than did their subordinates, in office as a private preserve, a gateway to power and patronage rather than a national trust. They thought in terms of responsibility to persons rather than to institutions or government. Thus Lord North placed great personal faith in his secretary to the treasury, John Robinson, Lord Sandwich in his admiralty secretary, Philip Stephens, and Lord Dartmouth in his undersecretary, John Pownall. That Robinson, Stephens, and Pownall thought to serve specific departments, or the government in general, in no way mitigated the private confidence the politicians gave them.[5] Intimate acquaintance with the great thus enhanced the subministers' normally influential position.

How influential was the position in the formulation of consequential government policy? Ultimate responsibility for policy decisions rested, of course, with the various heads of departments and with the cabinet. But did those heads arrive at independent conclusions and then consult subordinates about the best means of implementing them? Did they form only tentative ideas and consult their secretaries and undersecretaries before proceeding further? Or did all suggestions of policy come from the subministers? Did the great men simply lend official sanction to secretarial proposals?

Answers to these questions would measure subministerial influence and offer new light on the process of

[5] Such a situation, however, could finish, with bitterness and acrimony, long-standing personal friendships. Only the imminence of death brought North to forgive Robinson, so many years his trusted subordinate at the treasury, for his helping the king to defeat the Fox-North coalition in the general election of 1784 in order to insure a Pitt ministry. "And yet," Sir Lewis Namier argues, "thinking in present-day terms, we can hardly condemn Robinson, who considered that he served the Crown and not the individual minister." See Namier, *Structure*, pp. 37-38.

9

policy making in the eighteenth century. Answers seem especially required in order to understand those changes in British colonial policy and their most startling result, the American Revolution, that shook the latter half of the eighteenth century. Before then Britain's reasonably successful political, military, diplomatic, and colonial policies changed little. With a few exceptions the period from Sir Robert Walpole to the dismissal of Pitt the Elder saw no drastic alteration in the tranquility and orderliness (or disorderliness) of the system. George III's reign broke the spell. Britain entered upon a course of action that lost her the American colonies and brought far-reaching consequences in domestic, foreign, and imperial policy.

Who was responsible for this loss? Who proposed the British policies that led to the American Revolution? The first, most obvious, and most general answer is that the successive ministries from Grenville to North conceived and passed the legislation. Important measures such as the Sugar Act, Stamp Act, Townshend Duties, and Boston Port Bill may ultimately be attributed to the most important ministers in power at the time of parliamentary enactment. Yet crediting men in power with responsibility for a measure explains it only superficially, for it fails to consider the advice and help they received from others. Did George Grenville, for example, decide upon Sugar and Stamp acts in 1764 and consult his subordinates about the best means of implementing such taxes? Did he form only a tentative scheme to tax America and then ask his treasury secretaries how to go about it? Did they then suggest Sugar and Stamp acts, draft the measures, and submit them to their chief for parliamentary approval? Or did the suggestion to tax America and the explanation of the way to do it both come from subministers? Did Grenville merely lend official sanction to secretarial initiative? Was the subministerial role in Grenville's administration the same as that in later administrations, or did it differ?

Lack of the necessary subministerial papers perhaps prevents a detailed and final statement, but these "minor" men assuredly participated importantly—in at least four ways that have hitherto been overlooked or outlined only sketchily—in colonial policy during the era of the American Revolution. First, on a few occasions the subministers unquestionably suggested to their superiors important colonial bills. Legislation of some of these bills into acts of Parliament created measures that historians have deemed major causes of the American Revolution. Second, they often gave clarity and precision to, and formulated into parliamentary enactments, the colonial ideas of their superiors and other men. Third, they administered the colonial systems under both the old and new legislation, and could often interpret that legislation as they chose. Fourth, they attempted, in the center of administration as they were, to run the British war machine smoothly during the long years of hostilities.

The circumstances attending passage of the major causes of the American Revolution—the Proclamation of 1763, the Sugar Act, the Stamp Act, the Townshend Duties, establishment of an American customs board, the Quebec Act, and the "Coercive" Acts—dramatize the first three subministerial parts vividly. The merest glance at the complicated business of running the British war machine uncovers the fourth role. Of course subministers also shared in some of the countless minor decisions, matters that sometimes affected only one or two colonies, that contributed to the war. While the minor men can perhaps never be justly treated without a searching scrutiny of these areas as well as the major causes, the following pages do not chronicle countless minor decisions. They were often of a routine nature, but more importantly their introduction would only sidetrack the main study. Exploration of so many byways would inevitably lead the reader away from the forceful subministerial impact on major policy into a morass of petty issues and would cloud, rather than clarify, the subministerial role.

Secretaries, undersecretaries, and customs commissioners were not the only ones who influenced American decisions. Colonial governors, colonial agents, merchants, speculators, and hosts of other people were involved with British imperial relations. Nor were these three groups of subministers the only officials outside the cabinet to influence policy. The Crown lawyers and the legal counsels to various boards, among others, contributed their talents. Yet to narrate every suggestion or detail every legal draft that in some fashion found its way into major policy would pull attention away from the subministers. Perhaps legal counsels, Crown lawyers, speculators, governors, and many others need to be investigated thoroughly for a complete understanding of the American Revolution, but not for an understanding of the subministerial role in that movement.

The subministers dominate this study. Their place in the bureaucracy, their duties, and their impact on much of the legislation of the period through fulfillment of these duties form the main theme. The subministers did not alone cause the American Revolution. Their participation in many of the British measures that led to it, however, and in the prosecution of the war itself, highlights a significant aspect of that great event.

CHAPTER ONE

The Bureaucratic Framework

ONLY a few subministers significantly affected either the development of colonial policy or the prosecution of the war. Many departments and many individual offices—probably competently staffed—lacked influence because the ministry deemed neither the department nor the office generally important or importantly concerned with colonial matters. The British stamp board, for example, helped very little with the formulation of the American Stamp Act, though it participated in its implementation. Frustrated men in minor bureaus—as the stamp board—who hoped to suggest policy directly to chief government officials often chanced a hostile response. Odds favored adoption of their policy only if it traveled first to colleagues either in departments of government heavily involved in colonial administration or departments of government supervised by cabinet ministers.[1] Secretaries or undersecretaries to these offices alone enjoyed trusted access to cabinet members, or at least maintained a steady correspondence concerning the colonies with departments headed by cabinet members. Only these minor men could effectively suggest colonial bills, or give clarity and precision to dimly formed colonial ideas of superiors, or administer colonial legislation, or do all three. In practice those subministers who participated most in the affairs of empire—necessarily

[1] Henry Ellis, former governor of Georgia, showed how much he appreciated this trait of administration when he attempted to arrange an exchange of prisoners captured by a naval squadron. He tried to reach the admiralty through the American department and its undersecretary, William Knox, one of his long-standing acquaintances. See p. 68.

limited in number—belonged to only four of the many departments of government: the admiralty, treasury, secretaries of state, and board of trade. The customs board, also heavily involved in imperial matters, was itself comprised of subministers. In a sense the customs commissioners merely served the treasury as subordinates at admiralty, state, and trade attended their departmental chiefs. The customs secretary, himself a "minor" man, also worked for the treasury through subministerial superiors. Thus four departments directly, and one department indirectly, did the work of empire.

FOUR DEPARTMENTS

The first two of these departments, the admiralty and treasury, carried heavy reponsibilities. Official language of the eighteenth century perhaps best describes the admiralty's manifold tasks:

> to consider and determine upon all matters relative to your majesty's navy, and departments thereunto belonging; to give directions for the performance of all services that may be required, either in the civil or naval branches thereof; to sign, by themselves or their secretaries, all orders necessary for carrying their directions into execution; and generally to superintend, and direct the whole naval establishment of England.[2]

As the admiralty directed "the whole naval establishment of England," the treasury directed the country's financial establishment. The treasury board held ultimate responsibility for the initiation of revenue measures

[2] *Reports of the Commissioners Appointed by Act 25 Geo. III. cap. 19. to enquire into the Fees, Gratuities, Perquisites and Emoluments, which are or have been lately received in the several Public Offices therein mentioned* (London, 1806), 3d Report, 1787, p. 95.

in Parliament. It authorized payment for the armed forces, pensions, the civil list, and salaries to officers not granted in their instruments of appointment. It contracted with merchants for supplying the army both at home and abroad, for paying troops overseas, and with the Bank of England for the circulation of exchequer bills.[3]

To help them carry out such responsibilities, the admiralty and treasury had acquired over the years the services of various subordinate bodies. The most important office under the admiralty, the navy board, dispatched much of the technical business—timber problems, dockyard problems, new inventions, purchasing of ships—so vital for the maintenance of the navy. In colonial policy, at least, the customs board stood most prominently under the treasury. Although the English customs commissioners supervised the American customs establishment for much of the colonial period, the former in turn took their orders from the treasury and needed treasury endorsement for any alterations they wished to make in the colonial system. The creation in 1767 of an American customs board free from English customs supervision failed to diminish treasury control.

Other admiralty dependents—victualing board, sick and hurt office, marine pay office, and several more[4]—and

[3] For a description of treasury activity, see Edward Hughes, *Studies in Administration and Finance* (Manchester, 1934); J. E. D. Binney, *British Public Finance and Administration, 1774-1792* (Oxford, 1958); and Clark, *British Treasury*.

[4] Charles M. Andrews, *Guide to the Materials for American History to 1783, in the Public Record Office of Great Britain* (2 vols., Washington, 1912-1914), II, 1-9, summarizes the duties of these various subordinate branches. The eighteenth-century admiralty has received no detailed structural study. Only Sir Oswyn A. R. Murray seriously, but briefly, discusses admiralty administration in a series of articles in the *Mariner's Mirror*, but his work is not footnoted.

treasury subordinates—stamp office, commissioners of the land tax, and many others[5]—served only to assist the two boards. By their very existence they constantly demonstrated the impressive powers and patronage of the admiralty and treasury.

Impressive indeed were the powers and patronage of these two departments in the determination of colonial policy. Treasury, the most potent, directed the fiscal policies of the British empire. American finances—customs duties, American currency laws, reimbursement to colonial legislatures for wartime expenditures, payment of British troops in America—repeatedly challenged the treasury lords. Naturally, schemes concerning colonial revenue, from taxes to navigation acts, usually originated in the treasury or its subordinate board, the customs. Financial plans from elsewhere, in order to be considered at all, sooner or later found their way onto the treasury agenda. In maritime matters the admiralty dealt as often with America as did the treasury in financial affairs. Vice-admiralty courts, enforcement of the Navigation Acts, and protection of trade daily commanded the attention of the admiralty board. Occasionally admiralty and treasury jurisdictions overlapped, or at least complemented each other. If the treasury initiated plans to tax the colonies through enforcement of customs duties, for example, the admiralty's ships and sailors supported the overworked customs officers. The latter, in turn, often hoped to bring smugglers to trial in courts governed by admiralty law.

Two state departments, the southern before 1768 and the American after then until 1782, also dealt often

[5] The customs board, of course, possessed more autonomy and greater influence than the others, and is discussed separately later in this chapter.

with the thirteen colonies. Unlike admiralty and treasury these departments were headed by individuals, the secretaries, rather than groups of commissioners. Throughout most of the century until 1768 two secretaries of state, one for the northern and one for the southern department, managed British diplomacy.[6] Although geography determined their spheres of diplomatic responsibility—the northern department usually dealt with matters affecting northern Europe, the southern with those of southern Europe—they fulfilled similar duties. The southern department, however, in addition to its other powers controlled colonial patronage, except for a brief period when it went to the board of trade.

Perhaps the great authority of the secretary's department, even without colonial patronage, would have earned it a share in policy. The secretary of state corresponded with those men abroad holding the king's commission—ambassadors, envoys, generals, down to agents and spies. He ordered their movements and received their reports regularly.[7] His office apprehended traitors and criminals, and he pardoned, if he chose, men condemned for execution. The secretary could call out British troops and issue their marching orders. Since he was the most frequent correspondent with the king, and the channel for expressing his commands to other departments, he could often influence more than anyone else the monarch's attitude toward colonial matters. Control of colonial patronage, in addition to these

[6] For an excellent history of the secretaries of state, see Mark A. Thomson, *The Secretaries of State, 1681-1782* (Oxford, 1932).

[7] Some ambassadors also maintained agents at the secretary's office whose purpose, seemingly, was to search the meaning behind official instructions and sniff the winds of gossip. See, for example, Sir Joseph Yorke, ambassador to The Hague, to Richard Phelps, Oct. 4, 1763: B.M., MSS Stowe 257, f. 119.

powers, obviously fastened a secretary of state to the affairs of the western hemisphere.

The southern secretary's office relinquished colonial patronage to a new creation in 1768, the American secretary of state. The latter soon absorbed the American duties and patronage of the southern secretary, and it quickly assumed equality with the other state departments until its abolition in 1782.[8] Indeed, the American secretary's office dominated colonial policy in the 1770's. Endowed with the older secretariats' powers but few of their duties in domestic and continental concerns, the American department riveted its attention to the Atlantic coast.

Affairs of the New World also occupied the board of trade almost exclusively, although the powers it needed had already been parceled out to admiralty, treasury, and state. The plantation office managed colonial patronage during Lord Halifax's tenure in the 1750's but after then relinquished it to the secretary of state. Nevertheless, the board performed important services. It issued governors' instructions, corresponded with governors, and examined laws passed by colonial assemblies and submitted reports on such legislation to the king in council. Colonial complaints merited board consideration. The board examined accounts of all funds raised by colonial assemblies and expended for public purposes, and it summoned and questioned persons under oath. It employed legal counsel. The privy council voided nearly all

[8] Margaret M. Spector, *The American Department of the British Government* (Columbia Univ. Studies in History, Economics, and Public Law, 466 [New York, 1940]), is the best account of the third secretaryship. B. D. Bargar, "Lord Dartmouth's Patronage, 1772-1775," *William and Mary Quarterly*, 3d ser., xv (1958), 191-200, shows the department's gradual taking over of all colonial patronage, a sign of its power.

laws displeasing to the plantation office. Colonists of all sorts—Indian agents, merchants, speculators, colonial agents—argued their causes and cases before the commissioners and usually received impartial hearings and just settlements. According to the historian Charles Andrews, "the board was always willing to hear both sides of a case and at times postponed further consideration until all the evidence could be brought together, even though part of it had to be obtained, if obtained at all, from America."[9] These cases ranged from boundary disputes to land speculation and required special knowledge of every colony from Nova Scotia to Barbados.

In addition to its official work, the board performed an unofficial function during the eighteenth century. Its clerical positions trained colonial governors, diplomats, and exceptionally able "civil servants." Through them it exercised an indirect influence on colonial policy. The first secretary to the board from its inception in 1696, William Popple, resigned in 1707 to assume the higher responsibilities of a colonial governor. His grandson, Allured Popple, also stepped from the secretaryship to a governorship, that of Bermuda.[10] John Pownall, per-

[9] Charles M. Andrews, *The Colonial Period of American History* (4 vols., New Haven, 1934-1938), IV, 305. The best study of the board of trade is A. H. Basye, *The Lords Commissioners of Trade and Plantations, 1748-1782* (New Haven, 1925). Some information, not found in Basye, may be gleaned from the older and less reliable Oliver M. Dickerson, *American Colonial Government, 1695-1765* (Cleveland, 1912). See also Mary P. Clarke, "The Board of Trade at Work," *A.H.R.*, XVII (1912), 17-43.

[10] See Clarke, "Board," *A.H.R.*, XVII, 27-28, for the Popples and others who left the board for positions of grave responsibility. Perhaps the most interesting figure who went from the plantation office into diplomacy was Richard Cumberland, the eminent playwright who replaced John Pownall as secretary. Cumberland was entrusted with a delicate diplomatic mission to Spain during the American

haps the most influential of the board's secretaries, became an undersecretary of state to the American department. In that position, with over a quarter of a century's board experience behind him, he upstaged even his superior in colonial policy.

THE CUSTOMS COMMISSIONERS

The customs board, like the board of trade, participated extensively in colonial administration without important official powers. But the lords commissioners of trade and plantations exercised considerably more authority within their own department than did the customs commissioners within theirs. The latter always worked within the framework of treasury control. In this sense they acted as a group of secretaries to a more powerful government office. The larger office could hire and fire customs personnel, even the board secretary, alter given customs establishments, and direct all revenue decisions. In theory the commissioners merely carried out any or all orders, as would a board secretary. They enjoyed no more than subministerial status, and so their secretary might properly, though absurdly, be termed a "sub-subminister." The customs board thus stood uniquely among its four fellow departments.

The treasury allowed this unique body considerable latitude. It probably had no other choice, for the treasury possessed neither the time nor the personnel to master all the intricacies of the customs system. Many customs commissioners could unravel them with ease.

Revolution. His own account of the venture may be seen in Shelburne Papers, volume 168, William L. Clements Library, Ann Arbor, Mich. Samuel F. Bemis, *The Diplomacy of the American Revolution* (Bloomington, Ind. 1957), pp. 103-104, 172-173, puts Cumberland's negotiation in its diplomatic context.

E. E. Hoon, who investigated the customs department in detail, summarized the commissioners' work as "regulation of customs procedure; consideration of merchants' petitions; and formulation of customs policy."[11] Each of these broad areas involved numerous ramifications. Regulation of customs procedure, for instance, required the board to manage shipping and to account for revenue from the duties of shipping. The board selected officers for the discharge of vessels entering port; permitted or forbade landing of cargoes; ordered goods delivered from warehouses; specified regulations for the improvement of the service; commuted duties; transmitted treasury orders; created new regulations to meet new situations; and advised on points of procedure. The revenue commissioners enforced customs law in many ways. They decided upon prosecutions for seizures; permitted officers to search vessels upon specific information of illegal practice; maintained a coastal vigilance through customs officers and customs cruisers; and called upon the army and navy whenever necessary to help suppress smuggling.

The customs sustained all these tasks not only in England but also, until 1767, in America. All matters concerning colonial revenue—smuggling, the competence or incompetence of customs officers, the necessity for additions to or subtractions from a given establishment, requests for naval assistance—went to the English customs board. The treasury might hire or fire customs officers, it might determine new revenue laws and authorize new customs stations, but first it invariably sought

[11] The summary of customs duties and responsibilities is taken from Elizabeth E. Hoon, *The Organization of the English Customs System, 1696-1786* (New York, 1938), the best study of the revenue board.

the advice of its chief subordinate. Naturally, when the government hoped to tighten the entire imperial revenue system after the Seven Years' War it listened attentively to the proposals of the board of customs.

Proposals from departments other than customs, admiralty, treasury, trade, and state also affected events in America after 1763. Yet these five departments, either because of their intrinsic importance or their intimate connection with the colonies, unquestionably exerted the most influence. The subministers, to play an important role, necessarily would play it through service to these branches of government. The many facets of that service are keys to an understanding of the important role they did, in fact, play.

THE DEMANDS OF DEPARTMENTAL ROUTINE

The secretaries to the four boards and the undersecretaries of state performed similar duties. Seemingly endless and occasionally terribly complex, these duties immersed the subministers in all of their departments' operations. The minor men at one time or another supervised, or personally dispatched, every piece of office business. The demands of routine necessitated that they, better than anyone else, know the functions, powers, and limitations of their organizations.

Routine occasioned, first of all, that the subministers work with and supervise the inadequate clerical staffs. Many a secretary and undersecretary must have compared his pile of business to the number of clerks with dismay. Indeed, his staff was incredibly small by present-day standards. Toward the end of the century departmental rosters stood roughly as follows: admiralty—six clerks on the establishment, eleven extra clerks, and two marine clerks; treasury—twenty-five clerks on the establishment, seven revenue clerks, and two extraordinary clerks; secretary of state—often varied, but averaging from seven to ten clerks; board of trade—nine clerks; customs—several clerical offices of one sort or another, but in the secretary's office only thirteen clerks and one supernumerary, the western and northern clerks, a plantation clerk, and a clerk in the bond office.[12] The paucity of administrative help—even had all subordinates been highly trained, intelligent, able, and devoted to their jobs—necessitated that the subminister dispatch personally much business properly clerical.

Had the individual staff members been paragons of administrative virtue, the task of clerical supervision, at least, would have required relatively little time and patience. Unfortunately, many clerks lacked even rudimentary qualifications for their positions: departmental policies mitigated against clerical competence. The harried secretary or undersecretary rarely knew precisely what sort of performance to expect from a man newly entering his department. Initial clerical appointment owed much to connection, which could result in good, bad, or indifferent help. J. E. D. Binney's statement about the treasury—"in the absence of detailed evidence it seems safe only to assert that no clerk entered the Treasury without the influence of a patron behind him"—applies to all five departments.[13] That many of the subministers themselves had secured their initial jobs by this method in a sense argued for the system. John

12 *Reports of the Commissioners*, pp. 126-127, P.R.O., Treasury 1/470, ff. 33-34, "A List of the Clerks and other Officers of the Treasury with their respective Salaries and Branches of Business of the Clerks," and *Fourteenth Report of the Commissioners Appointed to Examine, Take, and State the Public Accounts of the Kingdom* (London, 1786), pp. 81-82.

13 Binney, *Brit. Pub. Fin. and Adm.*, p. 181.

Pownall, later secretary to the board of trade, began as a clerk because of Commissioner Richard Plummer's recommendation and also, probably, because Pownall knew Board President Lord Monson.[14] Edward Stanley, later customs secretary, must have used his influential connections to secure his first job in the service, that of customs clerk. His father had been a captain in the royal navy, and the Marquis of Granby interested himself particularly in Stanley's career.[15] But for every Pownall and Stanley, patronage tossed scores of uninspired and sometimes incompetent men into the hopper of administration. Patronage appointments—typical of eighteenth-century employment practices—rendered inevitable a clerical staff of uneven quality. Some men might be able. Others might be so bad that the minor men would defy cabinet ministers in attempts to rid their offices of incompetents.[16]

Even many of the unquestionably able and zealous people who entered the departments from time to time probably soon succumbed to apathy. Promotion in rank depended on seniority, not on ability. Each clerk rapid-

[14] *Journal of the Commissioners for Trade and Plantations,* 1734/5-1741 (London, 1930), p. 390. Monson knew the Pownall family well, for Thomas described him in 1754 as a "good & old friend." See Thomas Pownall to Baron Monson, Dec. 28, 1754: Monson Papers 25/1/44, Lincoln Record Office, Exchequer Gate, Lincoln.

[15] Granby described his early patronage of Stanley in a letter to George Grenville, June 13, 1764: Sir John Murray—Grenville Papers, file A 3. Stanley also told James West of an occasion on which Granby asked the Duke of Newcastle to promote Stanley. Granby "was going to the Duke of Newcastle, and promised me to speak to his Grace, and also to you, that if Mr. Wood died in his absence I might be preferred in succession." See Edward Stanley to James West, Nov. 9, 1759: B.M., MSS Add. 32,898, f. 200.

[16] The same Stanley later fired an incompetent clerk in his office initially appointed by the treasury. See p. 126.

ly learned that his promotion depended on the retirement of someone above him rather than the quality of his work. If nothing short of murder hastened that retirement and hence the clerk's promotion, a despairing but stoical attitude must have colored the approach to conscientious application. Many a subordinate might have asked himself: "Why drudge needlessly for an organization that appreciates old age instead of merit?"[17]

If promotion by seniority burdened clerical supervision, some exceptions at admiralty, treasury, and state hindered rather than helped. Their policies unwittingly fostered not only clerical indifference to work but active opposition to the secretary who exhorted it. Promotion to secretary or undersecretary in these three departments rarely went to clerks who had strained up the ladder of seniority. Even men who combined seniority with ability garnered only deputy secretaryships or chief clerkships toward the end of their long service. At the treasury the incoming first lord usually replaced previous secretaries and appointed new ones upon whom he could rely politically, taking no account of the pretensions of the clerical staff. The head of the state department often introduced his own private secretary into the office of undersecretary. While secretaryships to the

[17] A similar notion must have struck the treasury commissioners, for in 1776 they altered their policy of promotion by seniority in order to encourage better staff work. A minute of that year stipulated the following: "And my lords think fit to declare that in all future regulations & distribution of the business, they shall regard the ability, attention, care, and diligence of the respective clerks, and not their seniority, and that in their opinion this rule at all times hereafter ought to be attended to, and pursued, in order the better to conduct, and carry on the public business." This important minute advanced the principle of promotion by merit and must have encouraged some of the treasury clerks to labor harder in the future than they had in the past. See P.R.O., T. 29/45, ff. 27-29.

admiralty depended less on personal-political relations with the first lord than did those to the treasury, none of the first four admiralty secretaries in the eighteenth century began as clerks in the office. The departmental staffs, as a result, often resented the appointment of someone over them who had not secured his power according to rules they always were forced to obey. New secretaries or undersecretaries might expect, at best, grudging obedience to their orders and, at worst, passive resistance. Consider the plight, for example, of Philip Stephens during his early years as admiralty secretary. In 1751 the lords commissioners—with the obvious intention of grooming him for the secretaryship—appointed him second clerk over the heads of many senior men. In reaction the staff informed the board openly of its disapproval and implied the consequence, an intention to work as little as possible:

> We hoped that the number of years we had served in this office, as expressed against our names, and having undergone the fatigue and labour of the late long war, and as we believed to your lordships' satisfaction, would have given us reasonable right, in vacancy that might happen, by death or otherwise, among the clerks. But if your lordships should determine to put a junior both in years and time of service over our heads, it shews our hopes of succession to be ill founded, and must be a most discouraging and afflicting circumstance.[18]

The subministers, of course, could have surmounted clerical apathy and antipathy had the departments determined upon strict rules of attendance and conduct and discharged all who disobeyed them. Unfortunately, pol-

---

[18] P.R.O., Admiralty 3/63, minute of Apr. 6, 1751 (O.S.).

icy engendered frustration. Some offices never defined officially the hours of attendance until late in the century, and then posted easy schedules.[19] Even the admiralty—which needed someone on duty all the time to clear the dispatches that arrived day and night—did not, until 1745, in the middle of the War of the Austrian Succession, demand the presence of three of its clerical staff at the board every Sunday during wartime.[20] Since the boards expected such limited attendance they should at least have enforced it ruthlessly. Yet all departments seemed remarkably tolerant of backsliders. Only persistent neglect of duty brought dismissal, and the boards interpreted the term "persistent neglect" leniently.[21] The admiralty rehired upon petition and soon pensioned handsomely a man it had initially fired for being absent "for some days past" from the office, although he had been pre-

---

[19] The secretary of state for the northern department, for instance, required one clerk at the office at 9:00 a.m. The rest were not needed before 11:00 a.m. and remained only until 3:00 p.m. except Wednesdays, Fridays, and when Parliament was sitting. During these periods one or more members of the staff stayed an hour later. The secretary further used one clerk in the evening from 7:00 to 9:00 and three of his fellows on post nights. On Sundays a clerk worked from 12:00 noon until 3:00 p.m. The men supposedly served the extra hours in rotation except on Sunday, when seniority dictated attendance. See P.R.O., State Papers 37/13, f. 335.

[20] The following year, however, the lords aroused themselves and ordered one clerk to establish his residence close to the admiralty to be available for emergencies that might arise in the absence of the regular staff. The board allowed him 20 guineas a year from contingent office expenses because of the high price of houses near the admiralty office. See P.R.O., Adm. 3/51, minute of Sept. 9, 1745 (O.S.), and P.R.O. Adm. 3/54, minute of June 9, 1746 (O.S.).

[21] The board of trade dismissed men in 1727, 1732, 1735, 1741, 1745, and in 1764 fired several men at once. But in each instance they had continually neglected their duties. See Basye, *Lords Commissioners*, p. 18 n. 44, and *Journal*, 1734/5-1741, p. 190; 1741/3-1749 (London, 1931), p. 164; and 1764-1767 (London, 1936), p. 89.

viously admonished by the admiralty secretary for "notoriously neglecting" his duty.[22] Customs clerks expected reinstatement even if they had been found missing work for several months in a row.[23] The treasury, perhaps, indulged its absentees the most ludicrously. Its minutes record that Mr. Webster, "having absented himself from the office for more than two years past without leave, and it being understood that he went long since to the East Indies in the Service of the Company; My Lords are pleased to discontinue Him as a Clerk in this Office."[24]

If departmental policies unwittingly fostered apathy and neglect of legitimate work, they also promoted, again unwittingly, improper clerical activities. The subministers not only had to squeeze the proper services from their subordinates, they had to guard constantly against misdemeanors. No department, and hence no secretary or undersecretary, escaped the consequences of clerical mischief. Indeed the clerks seemed to abuse every one of their privileges. They were reasonably well paid,[25] yet

[22] See John Cleveland, admiralty secretary, to clerk Burchett, Dec. 26, 1760, and Jan. 5, 1761; P.R.O. Adm. 2/717, 38, 61, and P.R.O., Adm. 3/69, minute of July 31, 1761.

[23] See Edward Stanley to John Robinson, June 21, 1771: P.R.O., T. 1/486, f. 187.

[24] P.R.O., T. 29/52, minute of Nov. 30, 1782, quoted in Binney, *Brit. Pub. Fin. and Adm.*, p. 181.

[25] Payment varied in the secretary of state's office, but the maximum for a clerk was around £250 and the minimum £40. In the southern secretary's office in 1768, for example, salaries scaled from £120 to £40. See Shelburne Papers 134-147. Dartmouth, when American secretary, allowed his first clerk £250 and the other individuals of his staff from £170 to £40. See Dartmouth Papers II/1080, William Salt Library, Stafford, England. Although the four principal clerks to the treasury drew their regular pay from the fee fund before 1782, in that year First Lord of the Treasury Shelburne established each of them at a salary of £800. See Shelburne Papers 168. Each of the clerks on the treasury establishment received £100

they incessantly sought illegitimate sources of extra money. Sale of, or allowing unauthorized access to, public documents, for example, achieved great popularity among the clerks at admiralty, treasury, and trade. In 1740 a complaint to the board of trade averred that a letter from the deputy governor of Pennsylvania had been "lately surreptitiously obtained from this office." Suspicion fell on Richard Partridge, agent for Pennsylvania, who supposedly procured the letter through the connivance of a clerk.[26] Similar troubles plagued the board until 1764, when it attempted to enforce new rules of conduct.[27] The admiralty clerks encountered little difficulty in offering the same sort of wares to strangers.[28] For a long period outsiders secured undisturbed entrance to clerical chambers by lodging with the admiralty gar-

---

per year, while the chief clerk in the revenue branch of the treasury merited £400 a year, raised to £800 in 1776. See P.R.O., T. 1/470, "A list of the Clerks and other Officers of the Treasury with their respective Salaries & Branches of Business of the Clerks," ff. 33-34, and P.R.O., T. 29/45, ff. 27-29, minute of Feb. 22, 1776. At the admiralty the chief clerk earned £400 per year, the second £200. Annual payment for other personnel went according to rank and seniority, the lowest being £50 per year for extra clerks. For these figures, see Admiralty Secretary Philip Stephens to the commissioners of the land tax, Apr. 26, 1765: P.R.O., Adm. 2/538, p. 392, Adm. 3/48, minute of Aug. 31, 1744 (O.S.), and *Reports of the Commissioners*, pp. 126-127. Salaries at the board of trade, from £100 down to £40 per year, and salaries for men working directly under the secretary at the board of customs, from £130 for the plantation and western clerks down to £80 for the copying clerk, assuredly recompensed clerks adequately for their work. For board of trade salaries, see Dickerson, *Amer. Col. Govt.*, p. 22 n. 68. For customs salaries, see B. M., MSS Add. 33,043. See also *Fourteenth Rept.*, appendix 20, p. 112.

[26] Dickerson, *Amer. Col. Govt.*, p. 71n, mentions this incident.
[27] *Journal*, 1764-1767, pp. 107-108.
[28] See, for example, P.R.O., Adm. 3/49, minute of Feb. 15, 1744 (O.S.).

dener and securing keys to the garden, beyond which lay the clerical offices.[29] Even when the lords sealed this passage, the frequently ajar main entry doors allowed scope for private enterprise with admiralty manuscripts.[30] The treasury clerks proved equally ingenious. They multiplied their opportunities for vending official papers by renting flats in the treasury building to strangers.[31] Their customs counterparts found an even more lucrative source of income than the sale of government property. They acted as private agents for harried merchants trying to push their goods through customs. Clerks in the long room took the depositions of ship masters, surveyed exports and imports, levied duties, checked proper clearance papers, granted bonds or certificates, and completed reports to the customs board. Many merchants who lost their bearings in the maze of customs procedure hired these same clerks as private agents to manage their customs business. According to Commissioner Edward Hooper, clerks received more in fees from their anxious clients—some £800 to £900 a year—than they earned in salary.[32]

All clerks, save those of the undersecretaries of state,[33]

[29] P.R.O., Adm. 3/62, minute of Aug. 2, 1750 (O.S.).

[30] *Ibid.*

[31] See, for example, P.R.O., T. 29/37, f. 70b, minute of Sept. 23, 1765. The treasury commissioners hired a person specifically to gather and sort books and papers, the ranger of the books. He was to keep all documents "constantly ranged in their proper order." Yet the lords failed to achieve a permanent solution.

[32] Edward Hooper to Duke of Newcastle, Apr. 23, 1756: B.M., MSS Add. 32,864, ff. 385-391.

[33] These clerks did not receive fees but depended on salaries alone for remuneration. Until 1765, however, they enjoyed the additional right to frank letters. Parliament revoked this privilege in that year and, understandably, thereby created clerical resentment. Clerks deemed their services invaluable: only they could handle confiden-

abused their fee privileges. Authorized fees added significantly to clerical income. Almost any time any clerk in any department, save that of state, drafted any warrant, any commission, or any document for nearly any transaction, he netted a fee. In the month of October 1771 these payments alone brought each of the four principal clerks to the treasury £76 15s. 3d.[34] All fees—from the nearly £200 received by the clerk entrusted with customs work to the £5 going to the clerk allotted tasks affecting tower officers, the jewel office, and the salt office—were totaled and then apportioned to the staff.[35] Western and northern clerks of the customs garnered around £50 apiece yearly for their work in the quarantine service.[36] Commissioners who investigated the customs service estimated that in 1786 approximately £900 in fees accrued to the clerks working directly under the secretary.[37] Com-

---

tial documents and decipher secret dispatches. They therefore petitioned for reimbursement, cited their great losses, and recounted their previous attempts to win compensation. Their petition eventually resulted in Parliament's granting them an extra £500 a year from the post office revenue. Although the receiver general of this revenue then deducted the land tax from the grant, the treasury remitted the deductions. See Shelburne Papers, 134/105-117, and Viscount Weymouth to the treasury, Mar. 30, 1778: P.R.O., S.P. 37/24, f. 2708; John Robinson to Sir Stanier Porten, Apr. 24, 1779: P.R.O., S.P. 37/25, ff. 58-65; Sir Stanier Porten to Grey Cooper, Apr. 12, 1780: P.R.O., S.P. 37/26, f. 271; and P.R.O., T. 29/49, f. 80, treasury minute of Apr. 11, 1780.

[34] P.R.O., T. 1/481, f. 125.

[35] *Ibid.*

[36] P.R.O., T. 1/480 (f. 265?), "An account of Sums to be Allowed the Officers on Account of the Quarantine Service from 5 January 1769 to 5 January 1770."

[37] At any rate, the secretary took five eighths of the fees in his office, and these amounted to approximately £530. The other three eighths went to the clerks, but the total fees taken must have come to approx. £900. See *Fourteenth Rept.*, app. 7, pp. 81-82.

parable sums went to clerks at the admiralty and board of trade, and yet the clerks remained unsatisfied. By 1731 many of them at the board of trade had so grossly exploited their privilege that the privy council ordered the plantation office to post a definite table of fees. The customs secretary, encumbered with a similar problem, always maintained a table of legal fees in his office. The admiralty clerks even objected to a perfectly proper transaction between the admiralty secretary and the deputy secretary in expectation of securing all the deputy's fees and had to be officially admonished.[38] The innumerable opportunities for illegitimate income undoubtedly multiplied the difficulties of clerical supervision.

If departmental policies allowing misuse of fees, sale of public documents, indifferent work, and frequent absenteeism taxed the subministerial supervisory powers, those policies paradoxically must also have lightened the burden. Permanent tenure and promotion by seniority at least assured each subminister a pool of experienced senior clerks, even the dullest of whom would have familiarized himself thoroughly with office routine and acquired the capacity to handle normal business. If they were unprepared to meet new and extraordinary situations that confounded office method, the senior clerks rarely faced such challenges. Intelligence, ability, initiative, vigor, while admirable traits, could not replace experience. Even the secretary of state, whose staff consisted of several private servants engaged in public busi-

[38] When Secretary Burchett assigned half his fees in 1741 to Second Secretary Corbett the clerks protested vehemently. The second secretary, they argued, ought to relinquish the fees he had enjoyed as deputy. The admiralty upheld Corbett: the private arrangement between Burchett and Corbett created no vacancy among the clerks. The employment of deputy secretary remained "dormant" in Corbett. See P.R.O., Adm. 3/45, minute of Feb. 23, 1741 (O.S.).

ness, preferred experience to other virtues. He possessed the option of hiring, firing, and paying as much or as little as he chose to his subordinates, and he usually chose to retain his predecessors' employees.[39]

All the departments, furthermore, created special positions directly under the secretary or undersecretary to help with normal routine and nearly always filled them with senior men. At the admiralty and board of trade, for instance, deputy secretaries carried out the secretary's orders and helped him supervise the clerical staffs. The chief clerk in the secretary of state's office also acted as deputy to the secretary. At the customs, chief clerks shared responsibility: one specialized in business for the northern ports, while a second attended to the western ports, and until 1763 to colonial revenue matters.[40] The treasury established four chief clerks, with specific duties, to help the secretaries. It also enjoined the clerks to be prepared "to undertake any business that ... either of their secretaries shall require."[41] Thus all the subminis-

---

[39] Lord Shelburne, for instance, southern secretary in 1768, employed thirteen clerks. The oldest in service and senior in authority had worked in the same department 22 years. Shelburne, himself, had been secretary only two years. See Shelburne Papers 134/147.

[40] John Freemantle was the last individual to hold, at £100 a year, the job of plantation clerk in addition to his regular position as clerk of the western ports. In 1763 the customs board proposed, and the treasury accepted, a separate establishment for the plantation clerk. Freemantle, however, still retained his £100 a year to advise the new plantation clerk. See customs to treasury, Sept. 28, 1763: P.R.O., T. 1/426, f. 314; P.R.O., T. 29/35, minute of Oct. 5, 1763; P.R.O., T 11/27, p. 359, copy of a warrant dated Oct. 19, 1763; and P.R.O., T. 11/27, p. 365, warrant dated Oct. 19, 1763. The office of plantation clerk was abolished in 1767 when the American customs was placed on a separate establishment and Henry Hulton, the former plantation clerk, went to America as a member of the new American customs board. P.R.O., T. 11/28, p. 446.

[41] P.R.O., T. 29/33, pp. 218-219, minute of July 31, 1759.

ters in all the departments could always call upon experienced men to help them manage the staffs. Yet the expert help and experience could never compensate entirely for the larger problems. Frustrated secretaries and undersecretaries must often have bemoaned the time wasted in clerical supervision. They knew, after all, that more important matters usually beckoned.

All the correspondence of their departments took priority over a delinquent clerk. Subministers had to know the contents of each letter that came to their offices, for they alone determined whether they would answer it on their own authority or submit it to their superiors. "A good deal of responsibility," Undersecretary Charles Jenkinson noted, "was left to the under-secretaries. They opened the mail, circulated it among the ministers entitled to receive it, and sent it to the king—sometimes even before the secretary of state himself had seen it."[42] Any of the secretaries, substituting "board of commissioners" for "secretary of state," could have made the same statement. The minor men held equal responsibility for all outgoing mail, forwarding some letters at their own discretion and others at the command of their superiors.

Naturally, secretarial or undersecretarial correspondence concerned itself primarily with matters dictated by superiors. As Undersecretary Evan Nepean commented, "his business is to follow such directions as he receives, ... to prepare drafts of letters to persons of all descriptions in correspondence with the office, whether of the most secret and confidential nature or otherwise."[43]

[42] Charles Jenkinson, "The Busyness of Secretary of State," in Ninetta S. Jucker, ed., *The Jenkinson Papers, 1760-1766* (London, 1949), p. xi.
[43] *Reports of the Commissioners*, p. 12.

Yet all departments exchanged so much mail that neither the boards nor the secretaries of state could possibly have determined upon answers to all incoming messages, decided what business needed consideration, and dictated to the secretary all that had to be done. The admiralty's chief subordinate sent letters under his signature to all subordinate naval offices, including the dockyards; to admirals, captains, commanders, lieutenants, and even noncommissioned officers of the navy; to consuls, envoys, colonial governors, the treasury, customs, secretaries of state, board of trade, and many lesser departments. Even had the admiralty board met for eight hours a day every day of the week it could not have authorized all these dispatches.[44] Board decisions claimed priority in secretarial correspondence, but they contributed only fractionally to the clearing of mail from his desk.

Control of office correspondence overlapped a third subministerial function, the preparation of board agendas. The undersecretaries of state perhaps enjoyed less discretion than their secretarial colleagues. But the secretaries decided what business their superiors discussed during the hours spent at board meetings. Of course, any subminister placed the most important, most pressing matters before his superiors, but he often determined the important and the pressing. Business the incoming mail brought into the office journeyed from the subministerial desk onto board agendas only if the secretary deemed the items worthy of consideration. Any person who wished to appear before the board discov-

---

[44] Indeed, the regular board meetings during the century probably authorized—as seen in the board minutes—less than a fifth of the letters sent by the admiralty secretary.

ered the opportunity only after an interview with the secretary.

Preparation of agenda, dispatching of correspondence, and supervision of the clerical staff ordered much of the subministerial routine. The minor men, however, performed other tasks occasionally. They procured any important books or papers their superiors wanted, saw to their care and custody, and abstracted portions needed for study. They drafted commissions and instructions for officers their departments appointed, and they also shaped any board business to be considered by Parliament, including the framing of parliamentary bills.

If all these duties fell to all the subministers in all departments, each office demanded further specific commitments from its secretary or undersecretary. The treasury, for example, delegated to its chief subordinate the task of drawing up the contracts with merchants who supplied the armies. The undersecretaries of state —required to know at any given moment the exact whereabouts of the king—maintained a constant check on royal travels.[45] Their colleague at customs always explained customs regulations at length, seemingly, to anyone of standing in government, society, or commerce —from Lord North's lady friends who hoped to import silks, to ambassadors and lesser diplomatic officials who wished to exploit their privileges to the fullest, to East India Company merchants.[46] The board of trade secre-

[45] See for instance Sir Stanier Porten to William Knox, July 27, 1780: P.R.O., Colonial Office 5/43, f. 95. Porten informs his colleague of the king's plans to go to Windsor, gives the estimated time of arrival for the royal party, and further relates that the king intends to be at Windsor every Friday evening.

[46] See for example Grey Cooper to Charles Jenkinson, May 6, 1770: B.M., MSS Add. 38,206, f. 245; Edward Stanley to Thomas Bradshaw, Jan. 9, 1770: Joseph Redington and Richard Arthur

tary devoted considerable attention to colonial boundary disputes and the problems of colonial currency.[47] His admiralty counterpart soothed the perpetual rivalry between sailors and marines and often screened the many proposals for technical improvements that came to the board, from systems of signaling to improved diets for sailors.[48] Finally, each board and each secretary of state required that each subminister be able to manage, on his own responsibility, all necessary business during the absences of superiors.

Perhaps nothing summarizes better by illustration all the demands of departmental routine than one memorandum handed to Undersecretary of State Richard Phelps by his chief, Lord Sandwich:

> If Morel Diesque sends my wine as he intends by the first, or any ship bound for London, it will be invariably seized. Therefore pray write tomorrow to repeat to him to keep it in his possession, till further order.

Roberts, eds., *Calendar of Home Office Papers of the Reign of George III* (4 vols., London, 1878-1891), I, 2, no. 9. In one instance, customs board regulations for landing East India Company goods in Hamburg proved so complicated that the secretary necessarily explained them both to the king's agent at Hamburg and to the merchants shipping the goods. See Richard Stonehewer to John Freemantle, Oct. 3, 1765: *Ibid.*, I, 605, no. 1937.

[47] He also, seemingly, was responsible for the sanitary arrangements in the board's offices, for on one occasion he complained to the treasury of the "offensive smells, occasioned by some defect in the water closets used in the several apartments of the building." See *Journal*, 1764-1767, p. 24.

[48] The crackpot ideas that occasionally found their way to the secretary must have entertained him, if not have enlightened him. He encountered several proposals to turn salt water into fresh, and one suggested diet for sailors included what must have been a gastronomical horror, a marmalade of carrots.

Pray make yourself master of the Russian treaty of commerce, & of Ld. Buckingham's dispatch upon that subject, against I see you on Wednesday morning.

I depend on a messenger tomorrow as usual when the post comes in, as I expect letters from Cambridge that may require an immediate answer.[49]

Only one of innumerable memoranda, it tasked the undersecretary to master a treaty and remarks on it, prevent the seizure of smuggled wine, and forestall some clerk from misplacing an important message. It may easily be said of all subministers, as Mary Clarke said of the secretary to the board of trade, "every detail, from the misdemeanor of a clerk or the need of having a wall in the office whitewashed, to important matters of policy, was brought to the notice of the board by this same official."[50]

ROUTINE AND POLITICS

Part of the subministerial routine within the bureaucratic framework of each department, with the possible exception of the board of trade, included political work of one sort or another. Although some departments were far more "civil service" in nature than others—the admiralty far more than the treasury and state departments—and although some departments demanded far less political work than others—customs and board of trade less than the other three—few minor men escaped politics. The eighteenth century considered politicking a regular subministerial chore. That assumption accounted in great part for the insecurity of tenure of the undersecretaries and the treasury secretaries: incom-

---

[49] Earl of Sandwich to Richard Phelps, Oct. 22, 1764: B.M., MSS Stowe 259, f. 150.

[50] Clarke, "Board," *A.H.R.*, XVII, 28-29.

ing departmental heads naturally hesitated to retain men who had served their enemies.[51] Political subministerial work created bitterness between the prominent politicians who thought the subministers should serve them and the subministers who thought instead to serve government. Politics helped the careers of some minor men and hindered those of others. But help or hindrance, it stamped subministerial life.

It was an intense part of that life at treasury and state, for politics often led men into office and occupied a major share of their time once there. John Robinson and Grey Cooper, for instance, thanked their political ability for their positions as treasury secretaries. Robinson had managed elections for the boroughmonger Sir James Lowther and went to the treasury as a specialist in electioneering.[52] Grey Cooper owed his secretarial appointment in 1765 to his political and polemical abilities. Cooper, a product of Cambridge and the Middle Temple, defended, in two tracts of 1765, the Rockingham government against the written assaults of the Grenville faction.[53] Charles Lloyd, Grenville's private secretary,

[51] Ninetta Jucker states that the subministers retained office only by "accepting each ministry in turn as the unquestioned expression of their Sovereign's choice. The unwillingness of ministers to retain them was the only effective check on their transcendent loyalty to the Crown." See *Jenkinson Papers*, p. xiv. She is certainly right insofar as undersecretaries and treasury secretaries are concerned, but her declaration cannot blanket all subministers.

[52] William T. Laprade, "Public Opinion and the General Election of 1784," *E.H.R.* XXXI (1916), 224-237, first called attention to the vital work of former Treasury Secretary John Robinson in helping to defeat North at the polls in 1784. Laprade shed further light on the secretary's election importance when he edited his parliamentary papers. Ian R. Christie, *The End of North's Ministry* (London, 1958), gives a thorough account of Robinson's work.

[53] Cooper, lineally descended from Sir John Cooper, Baronet of Nova Scotia, resumed the title in 1775, some 140 years after it had

had composed a short pamphlet entitled *An Honest Man's Reasons for Declining to Take Part in the New Administration,* which condemned Rockingham, his followers, and the Earl of Bute, the supposed "magician" behind their appointments. Cooper waded into the melee with an apparent zeal for the truth and the Rockinghams. He answered Lloyd's insinuations in *A Pair of Spectacles for Short Sighted Politicians,*[54] and with a second polemic, *The Merits of the New Administration Truly Stated,* assured himself the secretaryship.[55] For his politicking Cooper earned a subministerial post and an annuity of £500 for life.[56]

Politicking also included duties other than writing.

---

elapsed. He matriculated at Durham College, secured a B.A. in 1746-1747, and an M.A. in 1750. He entered the Middle Temple on July 16, 1747. See B.M., *Athena Suffolcienses, or a Catalogue of Suffolk Authors with some Account of their Lives, and Lists of their Writings,* Vol. 3, *During the Nineteenth Century* (1847), f. 9. See also John and S. A. Venn, *Alumni Cantabrigiensis* (4 vols., Cambridge, Eng., 1922-1927), II, 390.

54 See Charles Lloyd, *An Honest Man's Reasons for Declining to take Part in the New Administration* (London, 1765), included in *A Collection of Scarce and Interesting Tracts . . .* (2 vols., London, 1787-1788), II, and Grey Cooper, *A Pair of Spectacles for Short Sighted Politicians: or, A Candid Answer to a Late Extraordinary pamphlet, Entitled, An Honest Man's Reasons for Declining to take any Part in the New Administration* (London, 1765).

55 *The Merits of the New Administration Truly Stated; in Answer to the Several Pamphlets and Papers published against them* (London, 1765).

56 Although according to the publisher John Almon, *Biographical, Literary, and Political Anecdotes of Several of the Most Eminent Persons of the Present Age* (3 vols., London, 1797), I, 92-94, the Rockinghams adopted Cooper because of his political ability, some men ascribed Cooper's treasury appointment to the patronage of Charles Townshend. See Charles Jenkinson to James Lowther, Sept. 26, 1765: *Jenkinson Papers,* pp. 386-387. For Cooper's annuity, see B.M., MSS Add. 33,056, f. 148.

Treasury Secretary Thomas Whately, for example, devoted more hours to the work of a "man of business" than to the drafting of polemics. True, as a pamphleteer he had defended First Lord George Grenville, the treasury's financial plans, and its colonial policy.[57] But as Grenville's man of business he did even more, for he held his chief's political faction together. He distributed secret service money and offices to the politically faithful; negotiated with his counterparts in other political factions; reported conversations to his superior; analyzed rumors; and weighed political considerations against administrative action—all while fulfilling the regular duties of a treasury secretary. Whately must have found life less hectic, if less exciting, after he lost office in 1765 and attended singly to the problems of the Grenville group.

The political work of undersecretaries of state might be as hectic and exciting as that of Treasury Secretary Whately. Indeed, at state as well as treasury politics alone prepared many a man for office. Only politicians became secretaries of state, and the government refused to admit until 1770 that the undersecretaries could be anything else. Before then the title and some of the duties alone gave the undersecretary an official status. In many respects he remained the private servant of the secretary of state, who, whenever he chose, could fire him and hire

[57] Whately penned two pamphlets during his tenure as Grenville's treasury secretary. The first of the two, *Remarks on the budget*, intended to refute David Hartley's attack on the Grenville ministry's financial plans in his work, *The Budget*. The second one, *The Regulations lately made concerning the Colonies*, coming after the Sugar Act but before passage of the Stamp Act, argued for Grenville's new trade regulations, condemned opposition, and advocated parliamentary supremacy over the colonies in the interests of Britain's and North America's prosperity.

41

a replacement, pay him, and permit him fees. Although the government established regular undersecretarial salaries at £500 per year in 1770, the political tradition of the position died slowly.[58]

Within this tradition politicians expected active political assistance from the men they introduced into office, whether their private secretaries or "friends" of political associates. Even those people without previous experience soon learned the twists, turns, and devious ways of eighteenth-century politics. Indeed, two of the more astute masters of that craft, Charles Jenkinson, later Lord Liverpool, and William Eden, later Lord Auckland, served their apprenticeships as undersecretaries of state.[59]

William Knox, perhaps more typical than Jenkinson or Eden, pursued a reasonably successful undersecretarial career dominated by politics. Knox, the son of an Irish doctor, started his public service as provost marshal for Georgia. He soon secured a gubernatorial appointment as a member of the council there and successfully introduced legislation to increase its powers. This achievement, along with other activities, brought him the governor's special esteem and enabled him to return to England in 1762. A year later he acquired the position of Georgia colonial agent. Fired by the lower house after writing in support of Grenville's Stamp Act

[58] For the regular establishment of undersecretaryships, see P.R.O., T. 1/519, f. 16, and T. 1/487, f. 293.

[59] For Jenkinson, see Jucker's introduction in *Jenkinson Papers* and *D.N.B.* The Liverpool Manuscripts—B.M., MSS Add. 38,197-38, 470—include the papers of Charles Jenkinson. For Eden, see also *D.N.B.* His papers, the Auckland Manuscripts, are B.M., MSS Add. 29,475, 34,412-34,417. Eden has gained some notoriety for the spy system which he operated during the Revolutionary War, and Carl Van Doren, *Secret History of the American Revolution* (New York, 1941), details some of his activities.

in 1765,[60] he joined the Grenville faction as its chief pamphleteer and expert on American affairs. Knox contributed an article on the colonies to John Almon's *Political Register* in 1767[61] and from 1768 through 1770 produced two controversial political works. One praised Grenville's administration and condemned the Rockingham government.[62] The second, intended to refute

[60] Knox's pamphlet, *The Claim of the Colonies to an Exemption from Internal Taxes Imposed by Authority of Parliament Examined* (London, 1765), defended Grenville vigorously and denied colonial pretensions to exemption from parliamentary taxes.

[61] Knox learned from the newly created secretary of state for the American department of matters concerning Sir Jeffrey Amherst and communicated the information to George Grenville. Knox then submitted the story to the *Political Register*, which featured it in the opening pages of the September issue for 1768. See William Knox to George Grenville, Aug. 20, 1768: William James Smith, ed., *The Grenville Papers: Being the Correspondence of Richard Grenville, Earl Temple, K.G., and the Right Hon. George Grenville, their Friends and Contemporaries* (4 vols., London, 1852-1853), IV, 334-337, and *The Political Register*, No. XVIII (Sept. 1768), 129-133.

[62] Knox consulted Grenville during the preparation of this first pamphlet, *The Present State of the Nation Particularly with Respect to its Trade, Finances, &c &c., Addressed to the King and Both Houses of Parliament* (London, 1768), but the two disagreed on how the colonies were to be taxed. Knox favored a system of requisition, to which Grenville was unalterably opposed. Grenville, however, approved the rest of the production. See George Grenville to William Knox, June 27, Sept. 11, and Oct. 9, 1768: H.M.C., *Report on Manuscripts in Various Collections* (Dublin, 1906), VI, 96, 99, 101-102, and Knox to Grenville, Oct. 4, 1768: *Grenville Papers*, IV, 368-369. *The Present State* so stung the Rockinghams that Edmund Burke, the Marquis of Rockingham's "man of business," penned a reply in 1769 under the title *Observations on a Late State of the Nation*. Burke's witty pamphlet controverted some of the statistics in Knox's tract, but while Burke admitted the need for financial solvency he failed to offer any constructive suggestions for increasing revenue. Knox's response to Burke, *An Appendix to the Present State of the Nation, Containing a Reply to Conversations on that Pamphlet* (London, 1769), accused Rockingham's agent of deliberate

John Dickinson's *Letters from a Farmer in Pennsylvania,* proved perhaps the ablest defense of parliamentary supremacy over the colonies of any work during the period.[63] His eloquently expressed colonial views were not incompatible with those of Lord Hillsborough, the first American secretary of state. Knox assiduously cultivated friendships in Hillsborough's department between 1768 and 1770, and in the latter year, with the help of John Pownall, secured a second undersecretaryship. In this position he continued to advocate a stern colonial policy through tracts favoring the Boston Port Bill and the Quebec Act.[64] "Politicking" had prepared him for the office. "Politicking" became part of his normal routine.[65]

That part of the routine was less normal, but ever present, with the admiralty secretaries. Although they enjoyed permanent tenure, and many of them had expressed openly at one time or another a disdain for politics,[66] political business always, turned up on their desks.

---

misrepresentation and stressed his failure to suggest any means of adding to the revenue.

[63] See William Knox, *The Controversy Between Great Britain and Her Colonies Reviewed; the Several Pleas of the Colonies in Support of their Right to all the Liberties and Privileges of British Subjects, and to Exemption from the Legislative Authority of Parliament, Stated and Considered* . . . (London, 1769).

[64] This phase of his work is discussed in detail on pp. 150-152.

[65] Knox is in *D.N.B.* His papers, deposited in the William L. Clements Library, are calendered reasonably well by H.M.C., *Rept. on MSS var. Coll.,* vi.

[66] Thomas Corbett probably represented the consensus of secretarial political views when he stated to his patron Admiral Byng: "If to acknowledge the eternal ties I have to you, if to mention your name with the honor I owe you be to be a whig, I shall so far glory in the name. Nor would you, I am sure, think the worse of me, if I bore the same respect for any benefactors on the tory side

The Byng controversy, for example, assumed major political proportions. Admiral Byng was executed, after court-martial, for negligence in failing to relieve Minorca during the Seven Years' War. The opposition in Parliament accused the admiralty of using Byng as a scapegoat for ministerial incapacity. The entire episode, they argued, underlined the government's ineptitude in the conduct of war. Under these circumstances Admiralty Secretary John Cleveland's work assumed political overtones. David Mallet, a poet, dramatist, and political writer, proposed to employ his pen on behalf of the ministry. When he called upon Cleveland for help, the secretary furnished documentary naval material. Then Cleveland, Mallet, and Lord Chancellor Hardwicke drafted a defense of naval policy in the Mediterranean. Mallet put the results into manuscript form and forwarded the document to Hardwicke. He remarked on it and passed it to his son-in-law, Admiral Anson. Hardwicke urged the admiral to reread the manuscript, check all mistakes, and deliver it to Cleveland. The secretary would then go over the whole compilation and, when satisfied, make a fair copy.[67]

---

which I should most certainly, had I the same obligations to them I had to you. These are all the lengths of party I know." Corbett further added: "I know no intrigue in business but honesty, nor any party, but gratitude to my patrons and to those who support me in the world." See Thomas Corbett to Sir George Byng, Jan. 3, 1712: Brian Tunstall, ed., *The Byng Papers, Selected from the Letters and Papers of Admiral Sir George Byng, First Viscount Torrington, and of his son, Admiral the Hon. John Byng* (3 vols., Publications of the Navy Records Society, LXVII [1930], LXVIII [1931], LXX [1933]), III.

[67] For the exchanges leading up to the pamphlet, see John Cleveland to the Earl of Hardwicke, Sept. 12, 1756: B.M., MSS Add. 35,594, ff. 191-192, and Earl of Hardwicke to Baron Anson, Oct. 10, 1756: in Philip C. Yorke, *The Life and Correspondence of Philip*

If the extraordinary Byng controversy transformed a naval matter into a political one, Cleveland faced less spectacular political business daily. He served, for instance, as intermediary between the admiralty and the Duke of Newcastle in regard to naval "jobs." Sir Lewis Namier illumined this aspect of the Newcastle-Cleveland relationship and illustrated the extent to which the duke relied on the secretary for pushing "place" recommendations.[68] Sometimes the secretary satisfied the patronage ambitions of politicians outside the admiralty better than did its head. In June of 1759 First Lord Anson protested to Newcastle against political influence in naval promotions. Although Anson would, if necessary, promote the duke's nominee, he harshly reminded Newcastle that "borough recommendations" harmed naval discipline. Sound method demanded promotion to command of officers whose ships had engaged the enemy at sea on equal terms, regardless of their "friends or recommendations." But Newcastle, undiscouraged, tried again in December. He requested that a "friend" be appointed to the vacant clerkship of the ropeyard at Chatham. Anson responded that the duke's letter had come "too late, the clerk of the ropeyard having been filled." Now Newcastle attempted a different approach. He recommended two men to Cleveland's attention in hopes that the request would reach Anson. The secretary, caught in the patronage maneuvering of a powerful politician, could only respond with a promise to do his best.[69]

Yorke, Earl of Hardwicke, Lord High Chancellor of Great Britain (3 vols., Cambridge, Eng., 1913), II, 354.

[68] See Namier, *Structure, passim.*

[69] Cleveland promised he would "not fail to mention Capt. Vane and Mr. Cook to Lord Anson, who I am persuaded will pay due regard to your Grace's recommendations, and I will not fail to

Special occasions might enmesh Cleveland, his predecessors, and his successors, even more in the web of politics than did the desires of pamphleteers and the patronage wishes of the great. Secretary Stephens, for instance, knew only too well the hard and determined parliamentary opposition to the Sandwich administration he served during the 1770's and early 1780's, for he drafted the lion's share of the defense Sandwich used in Parliament. Only the admiralty secretary could assemble all the necessary naval information.[70]

The secretaries to the customs also drew political work, although the central administration of the customs was more "civil service" in nature than the other four departments. Customs secretaries were invariably administrators risen from clerkships. Neither commissioners nor secretaries were members of Parliament. Yet patronage and political pressure still touched the secretary's life, before and during his secretarial career. In 1760, for example, Edward Stanley, clerk of the northern ports and future secretary, "pressured" a minor customs officer. William Temple, collector of Berwick, drew Stanley's fire:

From the connexion of office, and the intercourse we have had I do most sincerely wish you well, and therefore will make no apology for troubling you with this letter. I have heard from some of my friends, that there is likely to be an opposition about the choice

---

remind his lordship." For the entire Newcastle-Anson-Cleveland exchange, see Baron Anson to the Duke of Newcastle, June 15, 1759: B.M., MSS Add. 32,892, f. 96, quoted in Namier, *Structure*, p. 34; Duke of Newcastle to Baron Anson, Dec. 24, 1759: B.M., MSS Add. 32,900, f. 280; and John Cleveland to Duke of Newcastle, Feb. 23, 1760: B.M., MSS Add. 32,902, f. 352.

[70] This part of Stephens' work is described at length in Ch. 5, pp. 158-159.

of a mayor for your town at Michaelmas next, and, which I am sorry to hear, that you oppose Mr. Watson the present member. You know the having a proper magistrate may be of consequence in a future occasion, and though I am verily persuaded it is not desired that officers of the customs should interfere in elections, contrary to law, yet I submit to you whether it may not be reasonably expected that they should not oppose the friends of government, and whether your natural interest, and obligations should not hinder you from taking any part to his prejudice, and therefore, I hope, so far as is consistent with your station, you will render him the best services in your power, which, in my opinion, will be serving of the publick.

Since I have been in the custom house, I have known opposition of this sort attended with very disagreeable consequences. This I dare say will not be the case from the persons at present in power, but I can't help just mentioning of it.[71]

Thus one future customs secretary helped prepare that future by applying political pressure on customs employees.

That most of the subministers engaged in politics at one time or another does not signify that all secretarial and undersecretarial offices were political. Traditions and methods of appointment varied greatly from office to office. Obviously the admiralty—which never appointed a secretary with less than fifteen to twenty years of experience in naval administration, and granted him immunity from political taint—differed from the departments of state. Both the boards of trade and customs emulated admiralty policy, while treasury secretaries usu-

[71] Edward Stanley to William Temple, Aug. 23, 1760: B.M., MSS Add. 32,919, f. 258.

ally suffered the consequences of political defeat along with their superiors. But whatever the policy, eighteenth-century bureaucracy required not only administrative competence but political perspicacity from its subministers. Both talents, and the ascendency they might gain with superiors, largely determined subministerial stature.

CHAPTER TWO

The Basis of Subministerial Power: Bureaucracy and Personal Relationships

THE bureaucratic framework within which the subminisisters worked allied with personal relationships to superiors to form the primary basis of subministerial power. Nearly every chore offered opportunities to influence policy. If in addition a subminister secured the special confidence of his departmental head he acquired even greater authority. The secretaries and undersecretaries who attended regularly to routine were intimately acquainted with superiors and, blessed with their private trust, left a strong mark on colonial policy. So did the customs commissioners, for their mastery of routine itself inspired trust.

BUREAUCRACY AND THE CUSTOMS COMMISSIONERS

The nature of seats at the customs board, the structure of the commission itself, and its methods of arriving at decisions placed it uniquely among its fellows. Because the commissioners were subministers who had forsaken politics, they resembled other departments only superficially. Commissioners met regularly as a board to determine revenue business and received £1,000 apiece (£754 after taxes), a sum comparable to that paid other board members.[1] But these regular sessions and adequate salaries defined the borders of similarity. Customs commissioners, unlike junior commissioners elsewhere, harvested prestige from a bureaucracy that accorded them a civil service status.

[1] In addition they earned £200 a year from the treasury for maintaining the quarantine service. See *Fourteenth Rept.*, p. 112.

50

The Basis of Subministerial Power

That status owed much to the lack of a single authority within the department and a joint lack of ultimate authority over its internal workings. The customs board, unlike admiralty and treasury, counted no towering first lord among its members. All customs commissioners shared power equally. Unlike the often poorly attended admiralty meetings at which the first commissioner decided policy with a submissive echo from one or two other board members, the formal customs sessions often found all commissioners present determining jointly a course of action. A politician newly come to office could scarcely accuse the customs commissioners of following in the past the dictates of a politically undesirable board superior.

He could, however, accuse the customs' superiors, the treasury board and its first commissioner, of giving improper orders. Indeed, the political consequences of customs decisions invariably fell to the treasury lords, for the customs commissioners did not fully direct their own branch of the service at home or in America. Treasury ordered most major decisions and by right appointed many customs officers, up to and including the secretary and the commissioners themselves. Political responsibility, of course, attended this administrative responsibility. As a result customs commissioners could afford to approach revenue matters without political bias.

Statute further aided objectivity. By forbidding the commissioners seats in Parliament, it closed the only door to political preferment that bureaucracy had left open, contributing to a customs board whose individual members enjoyed remarkably long tenures unrelated to general elections or cabinet shuffles. Sir John Stanley served from 1721 to 1763; Brian Fairfax from 1763 to 1785; Samuel Clarke from 1694 to 1708; Sir Walter

Young from 1714 to 1731; William Hooper from 1748 to 1793; and Sir William Musgrave from 1763 to 1785. Regardless of the government in power the customs board would always have two or three capable, experienced members thoroughly familiar with the complexities of the department and the revenue system.[2] Secure in their tenure, respected for their experience, nonpolitically motivated, the customs commissioners could attempt continually to build a better service.

They could at times even defy the treasury when pursuing that worthy aim. Indeed, the commissioners often disagreed with the more powerful board over the training, hiring, and firing of subordinate personnel. In November of 1766, for example, the treasury ordered that a William Pike be instructed as a landwaiter at Poole. The order countered customs policy, and the commissioners so informed the treasury immediately. Customs Secretary Edward Stanley told the treasury lords that the board lacked any record of anyone's being instructed at Poole as a landwaiter for the past ten years. Poole, he added, was not a place of instruction in any case. Customs considered it "absolutely necessary" for landwaiters to have a "thorough knowledge of every species of goods imported," information not available at the port treasury had chosen. The customs commissioners, therefore, flatly disobeyed: they did "not think it proper that Pike be instructed at Poole." At most they promised to "give the necessary directions for him to be instructed at the ports of instruction."[3]

2 This long tenure and relative immunity from political attack did not mean that the commissioners shunned all politics. W. R. Ward, "Some Eighteenth-Century Civil Servants: the English Revenue Commissioners, 1754-1798," *E.H.R.*, LXX (1955), 25-54, illustrates in detail some of their political connections.

3 Edward Stanley to Charles Lowndes, Nov. 11, 1766: P.R.O., Treasury 1/445, ff. 245-246.

On a different occasion the treasury attempted to appoint jobs in areas traditionally reserved to the commissioners, and lost the lively dispute which ensued. When the Rockingham whigs took office and began the very jobbery of which they had accused their predecessors, their leader turned his attention to customs patronage. As first lord of the treasury he "requested," through Treasury Secretary Lowndes, the name of one Richard Higgins to be put on the preferable list of tidesmen for the port of London. The Marquis further asked that other vacancies on the customs list be left to his disposal. Customs Commissioner Edward Hooper immediately protested against what he deemed jobbery and flagrant violation of customs procedure. "Lord Rockingham, I dare say," Hooper averred, "has been induced to believe that what his Ldp. is now pleased to desire, is agreeable to the practices of his predecessors." Such was not the case. "No board of treasury, or first lord commissioner of that board," Hooper explained, "has ever (to the best of my knowledge and belief) broke in upon that right to the disposal of the preferable list in the port of London which the board of customs has ever had, and exercised." Hooper indignantly refused to transmit Rockingham's requests to the customs board.[4]

The obstinacy and conviction of the customs board in face of the improper personnel requests of Rockingham and other first lords indicates the influence it exerted. Nothing meant more to most leading politicians than the disposal of patronage, the master key to political support. Their allowing the customs commissioners to share the master key invited the inferior board to unlock freely the doors to the "lesser" problems of the colonies. Indeed, the customs commissioners in effect

---

[4] Edward Hooper to Charles Lowndes, Dec. 14, 1765: P.R.O., T. 1/441, ff. 423-424.

ments no junior commissioners stood even in theory between the undersecretaries and the secretaries of state, and the undersecretaries may have influenced events yet more than their fellows elsewhere. But all subministers, regardless of department, were more qualified than other officials in government to help fashion colonial policy. Few other men could hope to match their experience, and their accumulated knowledge must have contributed generally to their status. But their specific tasks—the supervision of all correspondence, the preparation of agendas, and their powers to act in the absence of superiors—even more than the general respect accorded them nourished their authority.

The first of these tasks, supervision of correspondence, propelled the secretaries and undersecretaries to countless minor decisions every day. Public officials who served a particular department understood letters signed by the secretary or undersecretary to that department to express its wishes. They assumed, of course, that the subminister merely relayed to them the decisions of superiors.[7] In many instances they were correct, but often

---

only £775 and £97 for coals and candles. While the secretary's income varied, Secretary Stephens estimated in 1785 that he earned, from various sources, £2,146 8s. 8d. See *Reports of the Commissioners*, p. 97. The first lord of the treasury received a salary of £1,600 and an additional £3,000 a year from the secret service fund. The junior lords received only £1,600. Although the treasury secretaries received no fixed salary they earned between £2,000 and £5,000 from the fee fund alone. The secretaries further received a share of New Year's gifts amounting to several hundred pounds. When Shelburne wished to end the fee system and fix definite secretarial salaries, he chose £3,000 as the most equitable salary. See Binney, *Brit. Pub. Fin. and Adm.*, p. 170.

[7] The admiralty reaffirmed the official authority of the secretary's letter when it received an astounding communication in 1743 from one Captain Hamilton of the *Augusta*. The Captain had found

the subminister dispatched matters on his own authority. Commissioners or secretaries of state could never catch up with all the business needing attention, so they necessarily left several departmental matters to subordinates. The admiralty lords, for instance, early in the eighteenth century realized the impossibility of discussing during their meetings the hundreds of matters demanding attention. They devoted themselves, therefore, primarily to instructing the navy board and its officers, authorizing promotions, examining lieutenants, considering requests for leave, and discussing important matters referred to them by other departments of government. Much of the other business they left to their secretary and gradually permitted him more and more discretion. The commissioners signed orders, but they allowed the secretary to forward the orders at the time he deemed most proper. As early as 1727 the lords empowered him to act upon urgent matters after consulting only one lord commissioner. In 1740 they further extended his authority by resolving that extracts of any letters from admirals abroad requesting stores and provisions be sent by the secretary to the proper office immediately, "without expecting particular orders from the board for it."[8] By the time of the American Revolution the board was apparently leaving to its secretary the right to grant admiralty passes to protect shipping from Algerian pi-

---

fault with one of the secretary's letters "as being too much in the stile of an order from the lords." The commissioners rebuked Hamilton for his "unreasonable remark" and declared that "every expression of the secry's public letters always contains or implied their ldps. orders, & is capable of no other meaning, & has been always so understood by the officers of the navy." See P.R.O., Adm. 3/47, minute of Jan. 7, 1743 (O.S.).

[8] P.R.O., Adm. 3/45, minute of Dec. 16, 1740 (O.S.).

rates and admiralty licenses for ships supplying the army in America.[9] Other secretaries and undersecretaries, it should be added, enjoyed similar authority.

The supervision of correspondence also enabled subministers to reach out, to cross the confines of their own offices and influence policy by cooperating with their colleagues in other departments. Indeed, informal exchanges between the minor men often achieved more than formal missives, supposedly authorized by superiors. Treasury Secretary Samuel Martin, for instance, unofficially hastened an important American sailing.

In August of 1759 he informed Admiralty Secretary John Cleveland that the agent for Massachusetts had £20,000 in Spanish and Portuguese specie requiring immediate shipment to the colonies. The money, a parliamentary reimbursement to Massachusetts for the cost of provisions supplied by the Bay Colony to its forces in 1756, was desperately needed for circulation in North America. "I thought it right to acquaint you with Mr. Bollan's [the agent's] information in my own name," Martin explained, "as I have not an opportunity of consulting the lords of the treasury." He exhorted Cleveland to order the specie placed aboard a ship for New York and to direct the captain to proceed from there to Boston with it. Cleveland willingly complied.[10] Two

[9] Although both these types of documents carried the signatures of the lords commissioners, they were invalid unless countersigned by the secretary. The necessity for the latter's name on the pass suggests that many blanks were placed before the lords to sign without particulars included, and that these particulars would be left to the secretary to fill in when the occasion arose. He could then countersign the paper and forward it to the proper person.

[10] See Samuel Martin to John Cleveland, Aug. 2, 1759: P.R.O., Adm. 1/4286, and Stephens (who evidently took over the job) to Captain Faulkner, Aug. 27, 1759: P.R.O., Adm. 2/713, p. 104.

subministers, on their own, thus successfully implemented a part of the government's colonial arrangements.

Another part of those arrangements touched the perennial problem of smuggling. Again, unofficial subministerial cooperation might lead, if not to its suppression, at least to the capture of some of its more notorious practitioners.

In 1757, for instance, Customs Secretary William Wood informed John Cleveland that several ships in a convoy for the West Indies had left their escorts, sailed to St. Eustatius, and landed twenty thousand barrels of beef. This meat immediately supplied the French men-of-war at Martinique and St. Domingue, "without which," Wood believed, "they would not have been able to put to sea." He asked Cleveland to procure a schedule of the crafts in the convoy from its commander, Captain Holwell. The list should distinguish between those vessels that remained in convoy and those that left. Armed with the information, Wood could "trace the matter as it deserves." Cleveland cooperated. He immediately assigned a clerk to the matter, and within five days Wood received his muster.[11] The customs secretary thanked his colleague for the help, noted that the names of the wayward ships had been checked against Lloyd's register, and promised to forward all particulars to the admiralty. "In the mean time," Wood hastened to add, "I beg leave to observe, that I did not take this matter up as a secretary to the commissioner of the customs, but was moved to it by a private letter which I had received from a gentleman of Barbadoes."[12]

[11] See William Wood to John Cleveland, Oct. 28, 1757: P.R.O., Adm. 1/3866, and Cleveland to Wood, Nov. 3, 1757: P.R.O., Adm. 2/521, p. 112.

[12] William Wood to John Cleveland, Nov. 5, 1757: P.R.O., Adm. 1/3866.

Another instance of illegal shipping prompted Treasury Secretary Charles Jenkinson and Admiralty Secretary Philip Stephens to an even more decisive response. Jenkinson told his colleague of a ship bound from Gothenburg to Guernsey loaded with tea and East India goods. The treasury secretary thought that a naval sloop might lie off Guernsey and intercept the merchantman, should it attempt to smuggle its cargo onto the island. Stephens acted at once. Officially he wrote that the sloop *Fly* had been ordered to cruise off Guernsey for the purpose of stopping any smuggling attempts. Unofficially, he added a postscript in his own hand: "If any information had been recd. of the time it was expected the *Pigeon* wod. sail from Gottenburg, or may probably arrive at Guernsey, you will please communicate it to me, that the time for the *Fly* to cruise off the latter may be limited accordingly."[13] Supposedly, a private note to Stephens would prompt secretarial altering of the *Fly*'s sailing orders, a duty normally expected of the lords commissioners. But smugglers did not await board decisions, and subministerial effectiveness depended on prompt and willing unofficial cooperation.

Prompt and willing unofficial cooperation through informal interoffice correspondence had become a subministerial habit by 1763. Departmental heads, of course, realized its effectiveness and sanctioned its continuance. During the next twenty years it would assume great importance, for many governmental colonial policies might depend on informal subministerial exchanges. These policies, it is true, would involve colonial currency and navigation as had the old ones, but in a different and vastly more consequential fashion. The new

[13] Philip Stephens to Charles Jenkinson, Apr. 23, 1764: P.R.O., T. 1/434, ff. 43-44.

approaches to colonial revenue and commerce after 1763 would help bring on the American Revolution, and the essential role of minor men in correspondence would guarantee them a share in the movement.

Responsibility for preparation of agendas would add to the guarantee. This responsibility enabled subministers to determine what business their chiefs discussed and in what order. In some ways it even allowed them to determine the outcome of board decisions, as did Treasury Secretary Grey Cooper in a matter affecting colonial revenue in 1773. In that year the merchants of Poole and Dartmouth trading to Newfoundland complained to the treasury of exorbitant fees squeezed from hapless victims by customs officers at St. John's. The collector there repudiated these accusations, and the complainants determined to answer his rebuttal. Lord Howe, acting for the men of commerce, handed to Cooper at the secretary's house their countercharges. Cooper laid this paper before the treasury on March 16, which scheduled a hearing on it for March 30. Meanwhile the merchants became dissatisfied with their second petition and decided to rest their case on the original complaint. Howe consequently wrote to Cooper requesting him "to suppress" the second paper, "that the pleasure of the treasury may be taken in the original application of the merchants." Cooper must have complied. Although the commissioners initially had resolved to hear the merchant appeal on March 30, no traders from Poole or Dartmouth appeared before the board on that day.[14] The treasury secretary had simply left the matter off the agenda.

Had that agenda been as overcrowded as the board

[14] P.R.O., T. 29/42, ff. 219b-220, minute of Mar. 16, 1773, and Earl Howe to Grey Cooper, Mar. 27, 1773: P.R.O., T. 1/502, f. 11.

of trade's—which it probably was—the lords commissioners would never have marked the omission, for the secretaries to the treasury and plantation office often put more colonial matters to their superiors than the latter could possibly decide in one sitting. In one session of 1773 the board of trade minutes record that the commissioners read sixty-seven laws passed in New York and the legal advisor's report on them. Obviously, the board could not possibly have read all these laws in one meeting, much less Advisor Jackson's report on them. The commissioners may have scrutinized a few statutes, but they left the rest "to determination by the lower orders."[15] The secretaries, of course, headed the "lower orders" and determined the other laws. Their relationship to board agendas had given them that power.

Subministerial scheduling thus invariably colored the colonial decisions of the heads of government. Any minor man who selected the particular colonial petitions, memorials, grievances and other matters that his chiefs should consider shaped the attitudes they would assume toward America. He stamped departmental policy equally strongly, of course, if he simply presented such an overwhelming mass of material that his superiors had to trust many final decisions to his discretion. As relations between Britain and America grew increasingly strained after 1763, the agenda duties within the subministerial routine grew increasingly important. Often the subminister had the power to increase or lessen tension. He presented the pertinent information upon which his superiors were supposed to base their official judgments, or himself rendered those judgments when

[15] Ross J. S. Hoffman, *Edmund Burke, New York Agent* (Philadelphia, 1956), p. 78.

his superiors were unable to digest the materials he had fed them.

If the preparation of agendas and the supervision of correspondence daily impelled the minor men to independent courses of action, the exigencies of bureaucracy sometimes bestowed upon them complete responsibility. Indeed, when, like Secretary Martin, they corresponded informally they often carried the authority of their department without having consulted their chiefs. If their chiefs were not present, of course, they were the unquestionable voices of government. Sooner or later circumstances pushed all secretaries and undersecretaries into what Customs Commissioner Edward Hooper considered the gravest subministerial task, the giving of orders "provisionally upon such sudden and emergent occasions as sometime happen when the board is not sitting."[16] The subministers necessarily exercised this freedom with discretion, for they had sooner or later to account to their superiors. That they did exercise it often, however, is manifest. Admiralty Secretary Stephens, for example, in the absence of his board speeded the sailing of Captain Cook on his first voyage of discovery. When government authorized the expedition to observe the transit of Venus in 1768 the admiralty had no ships to spare for the venture. It intended instead to build or buy a suitable vessel and trusted the navy office to survey, with an eye to purchase, the available traffic afloat. Stephens ordered the board to begin searching on March 5. Success followed shortly, for sixteen days later the navy commissioners described to the secretary a "cat-built vessel" and one "of about 300 tons." He immediately authorized on his own responsibility the board's

16 Edward Hooper to Duke of Newcastle, Apr. 23, 1756: B.M., MSS Add. 32,864, ff. 385-391.

purchase of the craft it wished. The absent admiralty commissioners, he explained, would approve any decision he made. The commissioners did in fact approve, and artisans soon scampered aboard to refit the ship. Its holds swallowed the necessary cargo, and only four short months after government sanctioned his voyage, James Cook weighed anchor for immortality aboard the *Endeavour*.[17] A secretarial moment of decision had keyed the operation.

Treasury Secretary Martin expedited a sailing that scarcely filled blank spaces on the Pacific map, but Martin's action filled a vacuum in authority and insured continuity in administration. In 1762 the privy council hoped to release a merchant ship hitherto detained in port by customs officers. The council intended neither the merchant owner nor the trade to suffer further, but a new treasury commission had not been completed because of changes taking place in government. The treasury, lacking both the first and junior lords, could not of course officially order the customs to comply with the council decision. Martin resolved the dilemma through his private initiative. He informed the customs board of the incomplete treasury commission and enclosed the order of council relating to the ship. Surely customs would "think it better to dispence with the want of a formal warrt., and would speed the vessel on its way."[18]

Neither Martin nor his colleagues made many major decisions in the absence of superiors. Consequential colo-

[17] J. C. Beaglehole, ed., *The Journals of Captain James Cook on His Voyages of Discovery* (Cambridge, Eng., 1955), pp. 605-622, lists all the official correspondence between the various boards relative to the *Endeavour*'s outfitting.

[18] Samuel Martin to commissioners of customs, May 28, 1762: P.R.O., T. 11/27, p. 169.

nial policy emerged from the deliberations by boards and the secretaries of state after 1763, but the minor men often solved the day-to-day colonial problems on their own authority. Furthermore, if they reserved great business for their chiefs, they often submitted their opinions on that business. Perhaps their power to act alone assumed its greatest importance during the war itself. Many pressing matters could not await ponderous board action, and the subministers' initiative became vital.

That initiative—the right to act with full departmental authority—certainly enhanced the subministers' colonial authority. Combined with control of correspondence and agendas it earned them permanent places of power in all administrations. Some subministers were, however, more powerful than others. Some of them exercised fully their functions while others seemed unduly discreet. Those minor men who most strongly marked American policy interpreted their powers liberally. But often they did so not because bureaucracy gave them the right, but because they had won special understandings with their departmental superiors. These understandings weighed heavily in colonial administration.

POLICY AND PERSONAL RELATIONSHIPS

Custom and official policy in the five departments obviously permitted the subministers considerable freedom of action. If they suggested an appointment in the service or a change in direction they could always expect courteous hearings from their superiors. Yet private understandings between the subordinate and his chief often finally determined the outcome of subministerial recommendations. Any secretary, undersecretary, or customs commissioner in the confidence, respect, and friendship of his immediate leader anticipated a favorable response to most of his counsels. The especially trusted subminister stood supreme.

By 1763 a tradition of cordial relations had grown between the successive occupants of two of the secretaryships, admiralty and trade, and their first lords. The civil service nature of the offices, the personalities of the secretaries and the first lords, and many other factors contributed to a greatly enhanced secretarial prestige and power. John Cleveland, for example, secretary from 1751 to 1763, became especially close to Lord Anson. Cleveland prepared for the future when as clerk of the acts—one of the eight commissioners of the navy board—he cultivated promising officers through private correspondence. Cleveland may have anticipated the friends of today as the lords commissioners of tomorrow, for he numbered George Anson among his early correspondents. The future secretary must quickly have noted Anson's potentialities and desired a closer acquaintance. By 1747, a year after he had achieved the second secretaryship, Cleveland had also achieved that acquaintance, for he gossiped like an old friend with the now famous circumnavigator. Their discussions ranged widely over admiralty affairs, promotions, news of ships' movements, and the foibles of the commissioners.[19] When Anson became first lord in 1751 his long-standing friendship with Cleveland, who became first secretary in the same year, enlarged the latter's responsibilities. In September the secretary's assiduous attention to all matters that affected his chief delivered Anson from a politically embarrassing dilemma. The first lord had been chosen high steward for Plymouth by the mayor and al-

[19] See John Cleveland to Admiral George Anson, Sept. 6, 1747 (O.S.): B.M., MSS Add. 15,955, ff. 217-218. In June of 1750 Cleveland even offered to become Anson's tenant in a house at St. James Square.

dermen. Ready to accept the dignity, he learned from Cleveland the pitfalls of such a seemingly innocuous situation. Four aldermen, "who always opposed the government interest," had decided to petition the Prince of Wales to accept the honor. Cleveland intervened in time to warn of opposition intentions and the whole business went to Henry Pelham to be cleared up.[20] The secretary thus averted a potential clash between his chief and the prince.

These and other services secured "many favours" for Cleveland, which in turn encouraged him to an ever more active role at the admiralty. When the Seven Years' War erupted the secretary exceeded his role of administrator and began suggesting strategy and tactics, including an attack on Martinique.[21] Contemporaries soon suspected the pervasive influence of Cleveland in most decisions of the first lord. One of these contemporaries—Mrs. Boscawen, wife of the famous admiral—testified to the public belief. Angered because her husband endured the cold and tedium of channel service when he should have been at her side, Fanny Boscawen blamed the admiralty for not ordering him home. She condemned witheringly the entire board, but reserved her full wrath for the secretary. Writing to her husband, who had evidently expressed anger at some admiralty policy, the indignant wife scourged the secretary:

That Cleveland is angry at your anger is very likely, but that his lordship should adopt his secretary's resentment—that is surely unworthy and would tend to confirm a vulgar opinion that Cleveland is

[20] See George Anson to Duke of Newcastle, Sept. 21, 1751 (O.S.): B.M., MSS Add. 32,725, f. 196.

[21] See John Cleveland to George Anson, "Thursday evening," 1756: B.M., MSS Add. 15,946, f. 63.

lord high admiral. T'other day his son Archibald was
made a captain and John Cleveland [the secretary's
eldest son] told me Lord Anson had done it unasked
by his father.... The boy is but 18, I believe. This
looks as if Cleveland really had that influence which
people give him over our superior.[22]

Naval records evince the partial truth, at least, of
Fanny's testimony, for they show Archibald Cleveland
with post rank at age eighteen. His father, in a position
of authority, had heightened official power through private friendship.

Cleveland's successor, Philip Stephens, followed the
tradition. He served successive admiralty commissions
from 1763 to 1795. Probably his greatest activity as
secretary, however, came during the American Revolution when he secured the complete confidence of the
first lord, the Earl of Sandwich. Indeed, measured by
patronage alone his position under Sandwich rivaled
Cleveland's under Anson. For example, during the latter
half of December 1775 Sir Hugh Palliser, at the time a
junior admiralty lord, frequently visited the bedside of
an ailing Stephens. After one of his calls Sir Hugh informed First Lord Sandwich of Stephens' wish that a
Captain Wilkinson be given a ship in the squadron preparing to sail for American waters. Would the first lord
be so generous as to comply? Sandwich would and did
comply.[23] Great indeed must have been Stephens' inti-

[22] "Fanny's Journal, October 4, 1756," Cecil Aspinall-Oglander,
*Admiral's Wife, the Life and Letters of Mrs. Edward Boscawen,
1719-1761* (London, 1940), p. 209.

[23] Sir Hugh Palliser to Earl of Sandwich, Dec. 29, 1775, and
Jan. 3, 1776: G. R. Barnes and J. H. Owen, eds., *The Private Papers
of John, Earl of Sandwich* (4 vols., Publications of the Navy Records
Society, LIX [1923], LXXI [1933], LXXV [1936], and LXXVIII [1938], I,
90, 95.

macy with Sandwich if the first lord guarded patronage
so jealously as some of his detractors believed and yet
allowed a bedridden secretary to appoint an important
command.

The public came to realize Stephens' amity with his
superior as it had known of Cleveland's. Henry Ellis,
former governor of Georgia, attested to the secretary's
prestige. Ellis attempted a speedy exchange for French-
men, evidently friends, previously captured by a British
naval squadron. He hoped to reach the admiralty
through an old acquaintance, William Knox, undersecretary of state to the American department. "Having
no interest at the admiralty," Ellis explained, "I apply
to you, hoping that the thing will not be difficult or
very embarrassing to you. Mr. Cressener[24] has also written to Lord Sandwich, but I must say I expect more
effect from a few words of yours to Mr. Stephens."[25]

If by a "few words" to his superior he secured pris-
oner exchanges and ship commands, Stephens enjoyed
more than normal influence. Times of crisis heightened
his importance. The countless demands of the Revolutionary War—sailing instructions, fleet dispositions,
emergency dockyard repairs, ship appointments, supplies—called for immediate action. They could not wait
for the decisions of a first lord who might be in the
country or someplace other than Whitehall. Courier-
ridden horses could not gallop fast enough to Hinching-
brooke (Sandwich's country estate) and back to meet
the sailing schedules of vessels dependent on wind and
tide. Necessarily, the secretary often acted alone. Philip

[24] George Cressener, minister plenipotentiary to the Elector of
Cologne, Trier, and the Circle of Westphalia, residing at Bonn,
1773-1781.
[25] Henry Ellis to William Knox, Aug. 20, 1780: H.M.C., *Rept. on
MSS var. Coll.*, vi, 169.

Stephens did not fear to do so. He moved forcefully, secure in the approval of his first lord. That approval enabled him to contribute importantly to the execution of the American War.

His counterpart at the board of trade, John Pownall, contributed much to the decisions that engendered the conflict. The office of board of trade secretary, like that of admiralty, tended to give the holder who wished it the special confidence of the board chief. But, as at admiralty, the secretary's initiative often measured the closeness between superior and subminister, and hence the extent of secretarial influence. The Popples, William and his grandson Allured, who at different times served as secretaries early in the century, enjoyed the particular esteem of superiors and eventually secured colonial governorships.[26] Although Pownall's predecessor, Thomas Hill, does not seem to have captivated the first lords of trade, John Pownall emulated the Popples. He carved a special niche for himself in public business, from his tenure as joint secretary with Hill in 1753 until his resignation at the beginning of the Revolution.[27] A second office he acquired in 1768, undersecretary of state to the American department, enlarged the niche. It helped him even more than his secretaryship to cement his ties with the great and powerful.

Pownall, evidently, was able to command the absolute loyalty of his successive superiors. The few measures, for example, formulated or implemented by the board of trade during the Seven Years' War, if Thomas Penn

[26] Basye, *Lords Commissioners*, pp. 15-16, describes the careers of the Popples.

[27] Pownall, it should be stressed, resigned only because he found his duties too burdensome and wished a less demanding position in the public service, not because he lost favor with his superior or with the ministry.

observed correctly, owed much to John Pownall's sway over Lord Halifax. Penn wished to oust Connecticut Yankees who had settled in the Wyoming Valley of Pennsylvania under land grants from the Susquehannah Company, and he approached the board of trade. Although the commissioners gave him no satisfaction, he learned that "Mr. Pownall transacts the bulk of the business." He also discovered that Halifax often depended absolutely on the secretary's judgment in board decisions. Penn reported Halifax as saying, "Nothing was done or could be done soon in the affair, but 'till he had seen Mr. Pownall he could not tell me anything farther."[28]

Pownall so far transacted "the bulk of the business" that he chose some colonial appointments during the short period when the board claimed the right to them. Both Cadwallader Colden and Francis Bernard benefited from the secretary's attentions. The former, a prominent figure in New York, president of the council there and long known as the old man of New York politics, wished to become lieutenant governor upon the death of James Delancy in 1760. Colden urged his friends in England to press his interest upon Secretary Pownall, who might be "of great use." When Robert Monckton came to New York as governor in July of 1761 Colden received the lieutenant governorship. Pownall admitted using his "best endeavours" to secure Colden's promotion.[29] The secretary's "best endeavours" secured Francis

[28] For Penn's encounters with Pownall and the board, see Thomas Penn to Richard Peters, Feb. 21, 1755, and to Governor James Hamilton, Dec. 12, 1760: Julian P. Boyd, ed., *The Susquehannah Company Papers* (4 vols., Wilkes-Barre, Pa., 1930-1933), I, 229-230, and II, 36-37.

[29] See Cadwallader Colden's letters to Peter Collinson and John and Thomas Pownall, and John Pownall's letter to Colden in *Col-*

Bernard an even higher appointment. According to the Duke of Newcastle, Bernard, an old friend and neighbor of Pownall, became governor of Massachusetts because he "was recommended to my Ld. Halifax by Mr. Pownal, secretary to the board of trade, who knew him at Lincoln."[30]

Matters of greater moment than gubernatorial appointments faced the ministry in the 1760's, and although the board of trade's powers waned, Pownall continued in the ministerial trust. Lord Hillsborough, for instance, head of the board in 1764, described Pownall's "ability and extraordinary application," and a year later testified to his "real public merit."[31] The status he had acquired, through the force of his personality in office, would enable him to participate in the momentous policy of the 1760's.

The force of that personality brought him even greater intimacy with his superiors during the decade that followed. Indeed, Pownall needed that intimacy to retain his authority, for he soon entered an office that had never grown, like his board secretaryship, into the "civil service." In 1768 he assumed the duties of undersecretary of state in the newly formed American department, where personal relationships, far more than traditions of office, determined subministerial latitude. If the American department could claim any traditions in the year it was established, they were those of its fellow state departments. In theory, at least, it was their equal,

lections of the New-York Historical Society, 1876 (New York, 1899), pp. 30, 38, 109; 1921 (1923), pp. 307-308; and 1922 (1923), p. 58.

[30] Duke of Newcastle to Henry Seymour Conway, Oct. 22, 1756: B.M., MSS Add. 32,884, f. 158.

[31] Earl of Hillsborough to George Grenville, May 29, 1764, and June 25, 1765: Murray—Grenville Papers, file A 4, Hillsborough folder.

save that its business centered on America rather than Europe. But the extent of subministerial power in any of these offices—southern, northern, or American—depended far more on cordiality between superior and subordinate than in any of the other four. Instead of serving an official government bureau in an official capacity, the undersecretary of state (at least until 1770) occupied a semiofficial, semiprivate position. The demands of his routine were clear. His discretion within that routine was not.

If an incoming secretary installed as his subordinate a man unknown to him privately, or known only slightly, in order to please a friend, the new undersecretary aspired to little weight in the department. An undersecretary who barely managed to retain his job upon a change in administration also expected little consideration from his new master unless he could forge his way quickly into his superior's confidence. After all, were the incoming secretary a political opponent of the outgoing one, he would naturally suspect the loyalty of a subordinate who had served his enemy. The undersecretaries not fully secure with their chiefs notably failed to use the powers of their office to the fullest.

Consider Undersecretary Robert Bell in 1782. He had just learned that Lord Shelburne "was certainly to be secretary for the Southern Department," and he hoped to retain his undersecretaryship:

> I take the first opportunity to congratulate your lordship upon this mark of the royal favour; and at the same time to express my hopes, that I shall be honour'd with your lordship's protection and approbation in my office of under-secretary, which I now enjoy with Sir Stanier Porten, whom the King has

permitted to retire; and I assure your lordship, that I shall give my best attention, and exert my utmost endeavours to render my services agreeable to your lordship.

Bell failed to keep his job, but even had he succeeded, Shelburne would probably have entrusted him with little sway over patronage or policy. Bell, after all, had served an administration Shelburne had attacked often and bitterly.[32]

Men such as the timid and diffident Bell of 1782 rarely exercised the powers of their offices. Anthony Chamier, for instance, undersecretary of state of Lord Weymouth in the southern department in 1777, failed to handle even a routine matter in the absence of his superior. An English merchant who informed the undersecretary that an armed schooner had seized his ship off St. Lucia received nothing but promises. Secretary Weymouth was absent and Chamier stipulated only that "at his lordship's return your letter with the several papers inclosed shall be laid before his lordship."[33] Chamier thus took none of the several steps his office permitted him while his superior was away.

John Pownall, because personality begot power, fared differently. When he joined his board of trade secretaryship to his undersecretaryship of state he immediately basked in the full confidence of his superiors. The same Lord Hillsborough who had praised him so lavishly earlier became the first American secretary. C. W. Corn-

[32] Robert Bell to the Earl of Shelburne, Mar. 26, 1782: Shelburne Papers, volume 168. Shelburne was "not unwilling" to keep Bell, but the undersecretary feared the earl would work him too much and so asked to resign in hopes of a pension from the Crown. See Bell to Shelburne, Apr. 9, 1782, *ibid.*

[33] Anthony Chamier to William Crichton, Sept. 4, 1777: S.P. 44/143:122.

wall, aware of the Pownall-Hillsborough record, predicted in 1768 that the new undersecretary would "do ye whole business" of the new department.[34]

The next seven years fulfilled the prophecy. Pownall's tenure exemplified the powers an undersecretary could attain who enjoyed the personal esteem of his superiors. In 1770 Pownall interceded successfully for William Knox. The latter became a second undersecretary of state and helped distribute more evenly the heavy departmental load. In 1771 a mere hint from Pownall to Treasury Secretary Grey Cooper altered both the wording and content of a colonial bill in Parliament.[35] A year later, when Lord Dartmouth replaced Lord Hillsborough as American secretary, the undersecretary's influence increased even more. Dartmouth, more easygoing in business than his predecessor, needed even more than Hillsborough the cooperation, friendship, and advice of an established colonial expert during the increasingly troubled years. Pownall inspired such confidence that Dartmouth, as two events of 1773 demonstrate, allowed him almost complete latitude to run the American office. In August Undersecretary Pownall supported General Gage's opinion that John Campbell, commissary of In-

[34] C. W. Cornwall to Charles Jenkinson, June 18, 1768: B.M., MSS Add. 38,206, f. 60.

[35] On April 22 Treasury Secretary Grey Cooper informed Charles Jenkinson that Pownall wished to extend to America the pending bill for granting a bounty on oak staves imported from Quebec. Cooper secured Lord North's approval for Pownall's proposal and intended, if Jenkinson had no objection, "to let the bounty go to all America for the present and restrain it afterwards if abuses shall be found to prevail." The bill was accordingly altered, passed by both houses of Parliament, and signed by the king. See B.M., MSS Add. 38,206, f. 371; and *Journals of the House of Commons, 1770-1772* (89 vols., London, 1742-1834), XXXIII, 341, 348-350, 352, 355, 361, 399, 404.

dian affairs, ought to be subordinate to the authority of Superintendent Sir William Johnson. Pownall then informed Dartmouth of the undersecretarial opinion:

> I think so also and I cannot tell why I did not, as I intended, prepare his commn. with that condition in it. A letter, however, to him signifying the King's pleasure that he is to obey all such orders and instructions he shall receive from Sr. Wm. Johnson will answer the same end; and if your lordship is of that opinion I will get Ld. Rochford to take the King's pleasure accordingly and send a letter down to your lordship for your signing.[36]

Consequently, an official letter from Dartmouth to Campbell expressed the king's wish that all Indian officers in America should be subordinate to the superintendents of Indian affairs and that Campbell should "govern" himself according to Johnson's orders.[37]

Dartmouth acquiesced again in a second and more serious affair. Governor Tryon of New York had requisitioned troops to suppress a riot between New Yorkers and New Hampshiremen disputing their boundary. The undersecretary deemed improper the use of soldiers in such squabbles, and he therefore, on his own authority, detained the packet for New York in order to send aboard it instructions forbidding the use of the army. After taking charge, he informed Dartmouth of the situation.

> I have also a firm belief that your lordship will be of the same opinion with me, & therefore to save time I send you drafts of letters (& fair transcripts for your lordship's signing, if you approve them) as

---

[36] John Pownall to Earl of Dartmouth, Aug. 26, 1773: Dartmouth Papers I, part II/876.
[37] P.R.O., C.O. 5/241, f. 244.

well upon this subject as upon such other matters, on which it is necessary that the King's pleasure be taken. Should your lordship approve them you will be so good as to write me an ostensible letter desiring I would request Lord Suffolk or Lord Rochford [the other two secretaries of state] to receive the King's pleasure upon them.[38]

On October 14, 1773, an official letter from Dartmouth to Tryon forbade "that His Majesty's troops should be drawn out."[39] Undersecretary John Pownall thus decided some of the most critical matters of government. While he served the two offices singularly devoted to American affairs between 1763 and 1775, he was bound to influence the course of events. His relations with superiors, which had enhanced the powers of his offices, rendered inevitable his role in the American Revolution.

The power of the treasury secretary hinged upon similar relations. Although in the year 1763 the office could boast a civil service tradition similar to, if not the same as, that of the board of trade, personality had often gauged the power of individuals within that tradition. The trust Robert Walpole reposed in his treasury secretary, John Scrope, or that Newcastle placed in James West rendered these men formidable.[40] Less fortu-

[38] John Pownall to Earl of Dartmouth, Oct. 7, 1773: Dartmouth Papers I, part II/886.

[39] P.R.O., C.O. 5/1104, f. 448.

[40] Scrope, although sufficiently attached to his office not to wish to leave the treasury upon Walpole's fall, defied a parliamentary committee of secrecy that enjoined him to explain Walpole's use of secret service money. Scrope refused to testify. "He had laid his case before the King," the secretary declared, "and was authorized to say, that the disposal of money, issued for secret service, by the nature of it requires the utmost secrecy, and is accountable to His Majesty only; and therefore His Majesty would not permit him to

nate secretaries, such as Samuel Martin, fulfilled their duties and exercised the accepted powers of office. But their influence on treasury policy could not compare with that of their colleagues.[41] After 1763, when the

---

disclose anything on the subject." Horace Walpole remarked that Scrope's response put the committee in "great perplexities." Nevertheless, according to William Pulteney, no one dared oust the secretary from the treasury. He was "as immovable as a rock." See William Coxe, *Memoirs of the Life and Administration of Sir Robert Walpole, Earl of Oxford* (3 vols., London, 1800), III, 274; Horace Walpole, Letters, I, 239, and William Pulteney to Duke of Bedford, July 5, 1742: Woburn MSS, vol. VIII, f. 131, both quoted in John B. Owen, *The Rise of the Pelhams*, pp. 108, 109. West became permanently attached to the Duke of Newcastle. In 1756-1757 he went out of office with Newcastle for a short period, and he again left office with the duke in 1762. Newcastle tried and failed to find a place for West in the Rockingham government of 1765-1766, but West, because of his loyalty to the duke, supported the Rockinghamites anyway. John Brooke, *The Chatham Administration, 1766-1768* (London, 1956), pp. 286-288, notes Newcastle's efforts on behalf of his former secretary and considers that "the relations between the two men did them both honour."

41 Martin revealed how little influence he felt he exercised at the treasury in 1761 when he commented on his father's efforts to get another Martin—Samuel's brother Byam—into the treasury. "Introducing Byam into the treasury as a clerk," Samuel wrote, "is altogether out of my power; the appointment of clerks being the Duke of Newcastle's peculiar province, and this kind of officer being in such request, that he stands engaged for vacancies after one another more in number than will probably happen during his life. Preparing & qualifying Byam to succeed me, whenever I am removed to an higher station, if he is to be maintained at your expence in this town until these events happen will be in effect to breed him to no calling at all. I stand (God knows) little chance of high & easy preferment. Nor if I did, should I think of Byam's chance of succeeding me in ye treasury worth a six pence after all the pains that could be taken to qualify him. He must be in Parliament, must be qualified with £300 a year as well as knowledge, he must be thought capable of being useful in an office that will not endure any negligence or amusement; & what is no less essential than the rest I must have power to drag my brother after me into

lords commissioners abandoned the "civil service" and refused to continue permanent tenure for one of their two secretaries, private understandings became yet more important to subministerial impact on policy.

Although the most famous secretary–first lord relationship during the Revolutionary era was probably that between John Robinson and Lord North, other secretaries enjoyed equal confidences at one time or another. Grey Cooper, for example, seems to have acquired a footing with North nearly equal to Robinson's. According to that prolific memoirist Nathaniel Wraxall, Cooper sat on North's left hand during parliamentary debates and supplied the first lord, whenever necessary, with notes of previous discussions.[42] Assuredly Cooper aided friends and pushed parliamentary bills because of his special position. On one occasion, in order to please his friend the famous actor David Garrick, the secretary procured a leave of absence for Richard Burke from his customs position in the West Indies.[43] At another time Cooper secured an act of Parliament, at Garrick's behest, incorporating trustees into a society for administering funds contributed by actors toward retirement. Seemingly, only Cooper's closeness to North permitted such latitude.[44]

---

a lucrative employment & one of the most envied (so little are the alleys of it known) in the kingdom." See Samuel Martin Jr. to Samuel Martin Sr., Nov. 22, 1761: B.M., MSS Add. 41,347, ff. 109-110.

[42] Sir Nathaniel William Wraxall, *Historical and Posthumous Memoirs* (London, 1904), p. 297, introduction by Richard Askham.

[43] See Grey Cooper to David Garrick, Mar. 14 and Mar. 18, 1771: *The Private Correspondence of David Garrick with the Most Celebrated Persons of his Time: Now first Published from the Originals, and Illustrated with Notes and a New Biographical Memoir of Garrick* (2 vols., London, 1831-1832), I, 417-418.

[44] See Grey Cooper to David Garrick, Jan. 29, 1776, May 25, 1776,

The Basis of Subministerial Power

Cooper, and to a far greater extent John Robinson, functioned uniquely as treasury secretaries. They served a man often too amiably willing to let others handle necessary business. When a physical and/or mental breakdown incapacitated the "prime minister" during a critical period of the Revolutionary War, the treasury secretaries—Robinson in particular—even assumed (unofficially) many of his duties.[45] The attainment of so much power, though not typical, shows the value of the office. Most other first lords neither broke down nor paid so little attention to business when healthy. Yet a secretary who acquired the firm confidence and the personal friendship even of an extremely active, vigorous, and attentive first lord influenced patronage and policy on a scale only slightly below Robinson's.

Thomas Whately, for instance, impacted treasury business sharply because of his standing with George Grenville. Specifically through Grenville's "favour" he be-

---

and May 28, 1776: *Ibid.*, II, 131-132, 152-153, 155. The statute is 16 Geo. III c. xiii.

[45] Whether or not Robinson was justified in assuming such a commanding role—considering that he held a position outside the cabinet—has been the topic for debate. Herbert Butterfield, *George III, Lord North and the People, 1779-1780* (London, 1949), p. 119, dislikes Robinson's influence and considers that the Treasury Secretary in 1779 "sat like a spider at the heart of all the intrigues, bringing this and that man together, and suborning one member of the cabinet against another." Eric Robson, "Lord North," *History Today*, II (1952), 534, argues on the other hand that during the critical years of 1779 and 1780 North failed to formulate any definite policies whatsoever. Yet at this time Britain was threatened with a revolution in Ireland, was trying to quell a rebellion in America, and was engaged in a European war without a single ally. Stability of some sort was required, and the threat of a breakdown in government explained the cooperation between George III and John Robinson.

came secretary to the treasury in August of 1763.[46] For the next two years he served his chief as administrator, pamphleteer, and "man of business." So close grew relations between the two that Grenville allowed the secretary to share colonial appointments, an area of patronage that the first lord guarded jealously. So much did Whately wish to serve his chief honestly that he asked Grenville to find a "fitter person" than his own nominee for a customs job in America. The secretary deemed the man he had proposed, a Mr. Williams, neither active nor able enough for the collectorship of Newfoundland, the position he occupied because of Whately's recommendation.[47]

Whately's honesty, industry, and efficiency so endeared him to his chief that the first lord of the treasury allowed considerable discretion in treasury matters. In 1764, for example, a Mr. Francis Gare applied to the treasury for permission to import damaged gunpowder he had purchased from the king's war surplus stores in Germany. Gare hoped to remanufacture it for exportation. The treasury referred the matter to the customs board, and when it reported favorably Gare obtained permission to import. Later in the year, however, he had shipped into England 1500 barrels and, contrary to the treasury intention, had offered to sell it there for exportation to the colonies. Furthermore, Whately feared that the importer had also smuggled gunpowder and had stockpiled large quantities at the isles of Man and Guernsey. Trouble intensified when powder mer-

[46] See Thomas Whately to Jared Ingersoll, Apr. 1764: *Ingersoll Papers* (New Haven Colony Historical Society Collections, IX [1918]), 293, and P.R.O., T. 29/35, p. 151, minute of Aug. 24, 1763.

[47] See Thomas Whately to George Grenville, Apr. 11, 1765: Murray—Grenville Papers, Whately file.

chants of London began complaining bitterly. Under these circumstances Whately took matters into his own hands and wrote the following to Grenville:

> If you think it deserves examination, I will write to the commissioners of the customs to acquaint them, that my lords being informed of an intention to dispose of the gunpowder imported by Mr. Gare in a manner not agreeable to their intention in granting the licence, direct them not to deliver the same out of the King's warehouse till their lordships shall have had time to examine into the affair, & have given them further orders in relation thereto: or if this is not agreeable to you, you will favour me with your directions what other letter I shall write, & I suppose you would have summonses sent at ye same time to Mr. Gare & the other powder merchants to attend the board on the 4th Septr. You will pardon me if I suggest that I wish your letter to me may be an ostensible one & that you would give yourself the trouble of directing me the letter to ye customs to be written as from yourself on ye state of ye facts, without taking any notice of what I have taken ye liberty to submit to your consideration, as appearing to me proper. I had rather the whole grace should come from you, if you will only be so good as to throw in some general words to give me a latitude of adding what else may be necessary for the satisfaction of the parties concerned.[48]

Grenville subsequently approved every one of his secre-

[48] Thomas Whately to George Grenville, Aug. 18, 1765: Murray —Grenville Papers, Whately file.

tary's suggestions. As a matter of routine he trusted Whately's judgment implicitly.[49]

During the years of the Grenville ministry, 1763-1765, that judgment pondered weightier matters than powder smugglers. Yet smugglers and customs collectors related to stamps and sugar. Grenville mixed suppression of smuggling with hopes for an American revenue sufficient for the costs of American administration in his Sugar and Stamp acts. If Grenville granted wide latitude to his secretary in the affairs of Williams and Gare, at the least he expected in return Whately's devotion to himself and the important colonial legislation he hoped to enact. Because he secured devotion and returned it strongly to his secretary, Whately would participate fully in some of the most fateful American statutes of the Revolutionary era. His special relation to his chief would bring him to a decisive part in the disintegration of the first British Empire.

Personal relationships between the customs commissioners, their secretary, and the first lord of the treasury figured less strongly. Although the commissioners and their secretary often might, and probably did, maintain the same cordiality with their superiors that Whately did with Grenville, their personal standings were necessarily less decisive to final conclusions. The commissioners did not make policy directly, they only recommended it to the treasury. The civil service nature of the commission often guaranteed the recommendation a favorable hearing, but neither the commissioners nor their secretary possessed the same opportunities as subministers in other departments to become intimately acquainted with their superior, the first lord of the treasury. They worked in different offices at different jobs. Nonetheless, the occa-

[49] See P.R.O., T. 11/27, p. 442, and T. 27/29, p. 56.

sional customs commissioner or secretary who attracted the particular notice of his treasury chief at the least enhanced the consideration the treasury gave to customs board proposals.

Both Customs Commissioner Edward Hooper and Customs Secretary William Wood undoubtedly inflated permanently the prestige of the customs in the councils of the treasury. Their friendship with the Duke of Newcastle enabled them to acquire public service reputations which his successors respected. Wood opened a correspondence with Newcastle even before becoming secretary and continued it regularly. In 1738, when Newcastle was a secretary of state, Wood handed to one of the duke's friends a paper relating to Spanish capture of British ships and the subsequent posture of the British government. This first contact blossomed beautifully. By 1739 Wood could express gratification to Newcastle for implementing fully his plans for reinforcing the fleet at Gibraltar. The correspondence prospered through the War of the Austrian Succession and the Seven Years' War, when Newcastle became first lord of the treasury. Perhaps because of his direct communication with the treasury's first lord, especially over imperial matters, Wood came by 1763 to be revered as an oracle on American revenue policy by the ministries that tried to alter it.[50]

[50] Wood's correspondence with Newcastle is scattered throughout B.M., MSS Add. 32,691 through 32,892. The ministry consulted him about the new plans for gaining a revenue from America in 1764. He furnished some necessary statistical data, but he did not fail at the same time to offer an opinion against any new American legislation: "I wish that every [th]ing which may have been thought of respecting the Plantations may be deferred to another year. . . . For if what I have occasionally heard mentioned be true, I conceive you want information of several things from the Plantations."

Wood's superior, Edward Hooper, because of his relation with Newcastle and his successors, was also deemed an oracle in all matters pertaining to revenue. Hooper, like Wood, troubled to cultivate the duke, especially during the Seven Years' War. He urged civil service reforms in the customs on him, explained the entire revenue system, and recommended appointments. Newcastle, in answer to one of Hooper's proposals, generously declared that "nobody's testimony will have more, (if so much) weight with me as yours."[51] The "old" Whig, Lord Rockingham, who attired himself in Newcastle's mantle some nine years later, respected the commissioner equally.[52] Not surprisingly, Hooper's name would be prominent among the signatures of those commissioners who submitted recommendations to the treasury concerning American revenue policy from 1759 to 1767.

Many other men signed opinions about America during and after this period—legal counsels to the boards, the crown lawyers, American officials—and some of them unquestionably affected the final decisions. Yet Hooper, Whately, Pownall, Stephens, and their colleagues in the five departments most concerned with America exerted the greatest influence on the most important policies. Fortune and their ambitions had placed them in offices vital to administration. Through the force of their per-

---

See William Wood to Charles Jenkinson, Jan. 10, 1764: B.M., MSS Add. 38,202, f. 23, quoted in *Jenkinson Papers*, p. 254.

[51] Duke of Newcastle to Edward Hooper, Apr. 10, 1756: B.M., MSS Add. 32,864, ff. 218-219.

[52] Rockingham, perhaps, even thought Hooper dominated the customs board, for on one occasion he tried to secure a favorable customs decision to a treasury proposal by working through Hooper alone. He did not, incidentally, secure a favorable response from the commissioner.

sonality, through their friendships with prominent ministers, they had enhanced their prestige. A concatenation of circumstances singled them out to lead the last parade of the first British Empire. Their advice and opinions would govern the decisions that went out from Whitehall to the New World.

CHAPTER THREE

Five Years of Multiple Participation

DURING the five years from 1763 to 1768 the British government weakened the increasingly fragile ties with its American colonies. The Proclamation of 1763, the Sugar Act, the Stamp Act, the Townshend Duties, the establishment of an American customs board, and the general colonial revenue policy damaged relations seriously. Although tension eased between 1768 and 1773, the pressure of harsh British measures, resumed in 1774, toppled the bridge between Britain and North America. The first British Empire then slowly collapsed.

Subministers contributed largely to this structural collapse. Their essential positions at the treasury, customs, and to a lesser extent the admiralty and board of trade guaranteed their sharing in the imperial program. Their duties and powers—supervising correspondence, preparing agendas, acting in the absence of superiors—promised them a large share. Private amity with great ministers of state elevated a few of them into leadership, and all of them helped guide imperial destiny. They colored—in any one or all three of the following ways —every major piece of colonial legislation to emerge during the period: (1) They implemented policy by shaping into precise acts or proclamations the ministry's clearly outlined American proposals and by enforcing whatever parts of the new legislation properly fell within their departmental jurisdictions. (2) They formulated vaguely planned or only dimly considered ministerial ideas into acts of Parliament or orders to colonial officials. (3) Most importantly, on a few occasions they

86

actually suggested the colonial measures the government adopted.

Whether or not a subminister fulfilled more than one of the three roles depended on the subminister, or the department, or both. The enactments of the 1760's, with the exception of the Proclamation of 1763, related chiefly to revenue and invited the major participation of the treasury and the customs commissioners and their secretary. But the admiralty and its leading subordinate shared. Enforcement of customs regulations in America ultimately depended on the British navy, as did the security of the trade those laws governed. The customs commissioners had often relied upon the navy to support their officers in home waters, and they needed no less help in America. Although the board of trade possessed little power in the management of imperial finances, it had often been consulted about all colonial matters, including those concerned with revenue. The plantation office now figured in issues relating to boundaries, new settlements, and Indian policy.

Many departments called upon the board of trade secretary, John Pownall, for counsel all during the period, and his stature quickly grew. As undersecretary to the American department he would even arrive at a position of dominance, but his undersecretarial colleagues in the two other state departments played insignificant parts in the colonial drama of the 1760's. The state departments focused on Europe, not the colonies, until 1768. After that date the newly created American department of state joined the boards in dealing with America. Indeed, it soon assumed paramountcy and in the early 1770's, until hostilities opened, nearly excluded them from colonial affairs. But the 1760's, before

American department dominance, belonged to many subministers. They were years of multiple participation.

It is natural that some men participated more than others. Departmental lines crossed and crisscrossed, but those individuals who served departments directly connected to the new colonial laws exerted more influence than others. Subministers at the board of trade, officially at least, contributed importantly to the drafting of the Proclamation of 1763. The customs commissioners were prominent in the Sugar Act, Townshend Duties, and the general enforcing of revenue laws until 1768. The treasury secretary dominated the preparations of the Stamp Act. Lesser roles went to men outside these departments, the "experts" that government consulted from time to time. In the end, of course, many people helped the specialists prepare the legislation served to America.

THE PROCLAMATION OF 1763

If Americans found most of this legislation singularly unappealing, they accepted part of the Proclamation of 1763. It proved more digestible than the parliamentary acts that followed, but it awakened colonists to the possibility of an extremely distasteful future. The Proclamation itself officially determined a western boundary in America beyond which the colonists could not settle and regulated the Indian trade. It provided for a permanent standing army on the colonial frontiers and established the new governments in the Floridas and Quebec with stricter British control than hitherto exercised over the older continental colonies. Americans reacted less violently to the new policy this document outlined than they did later to the Stamp Act, but the Proclamation stirred American dissatisfaction with Britain, a dissatisfaction that had been growing because of previous British measures. These measures—instruction by the privy council to the Virginia governor regarding Virginia legislation, privy council orders relating to colonial judicial commissions, and writs of assistance in Massachusetts—were, however, piecemeal and did not formally, either by proclamation or parliamentary act, state official British policy. The Proclamation left no doubt.

Earlier historical studies attributed the origins of this Proclamation to exchanges between the secretary of state for the southern department and the board of trade during the summer of 1763 and ideas that emerged from among the board's staff. Three pieces of correspondence in particular—Secretary of State Egremont's letter to the board of May 5, 1763, asking the commissioners' opinions concerning commerce, forms of government, number of troops for America, taxation, Indian posts, and other pertinent matters, and the board's responses of June 8 and August 5—seemed to reflect decisions particularly important to the creation of the Proclamation. Board personnel who contributed to its drafting included everyone from Lord Shelburne, head of the plantation office when Egremont first queried it, to John Pownall, the board's secretary.[1]

---

[1] The letters and recommendations which passed between the Earl of Egremont and the board of trade are printed in Adam Shortt and Arthur G. Doughty, eds., *Documents Relating to the Constitutional History of Canada* (2 vols., Ottawa, 1907), I, 93-123. Clarence W. Alvord in his *The Mississippi Valley in British Politics* (2 vols., Cleveland, 1917), I, considered the Proclamation of 1763 a reversal of Shelburne's liberal ideas, a reversal that occurred after the earl had left the board. R. A. Humphreys, in his "Lord Shelburne and the Proclamation of 1763," *E.H.R.*, XLIX (1934), 241-264, denied Alvord's interpretation. Humphreys contended that the proclamation was the logical result of policies formulated when

More recent works have shown that while the board played a part in the Proclamation of 1763, the merely formal exchanges between it and the secretary of state had little to do with the drafting of the document.[2] Indeed, most evidence indicates that the proclamation did little more than incorporate into policy *ad hoc* measures adopted by the British government during the Seven Years' War. Furthermore, several suggestions reached the treasury in January, February, and March, before the board of trade ever acted, arguing for most of the ideas that later emerged in the proclamation.[3] Two months before sending his questionnaire Egremont provided First Lord of the Treasury George Grenville with a map of America that had forts and divisions of government clearly marked, "as according to the best ideas I have been able to collect, I should prepare for a rough idea of the new settlement of North America, & the West Indies after the peace."[4] That Egremont had already prepared measures is evidenced by his communication to the board in May, for his message not only asked for

---

Shelburne headed the board rather than a blunder committed by someone else after Shelburne left office.

[2] See Sosin, *Whitehall*, especially pp. 52-78.

[3] An unsigned letter to the Earl of Bute, Jan. 17, 1763: B.M., MSS Add. 38,334, ff. 297-300, proposes a regular standing army on the frontier, new settlements in the south, and regulation of the Indian trade. "Hints respecting our acquisitions in America," Feb. 2, 1763: B.M., MSS Add. 38,335, ff. 1-8, contain similar ideas. A document of Feb. 25, 1763: *Ibid.*, ff. 14-33, and another of Mar. 10, 1763: *Ibid.*, ff. 69-77, again suggest the same propositions. As secretary to the board of trade, John Pownall was aware, if not responsible, for restricting interior settlements in Virginia much earlier. See for example the board of trade's letters to Governor Faquier of Virginia in 1760-1761 in P.R.O., C.O. 5/1330.

[4] Earl of Egremont to George Grenville, Mar. 11, 1763: Murray—Grenville Papers, file A 2, Egremont folder.

board opinions but included a paper of "hints" suggesting what opinions the board should form. With only two exceptions—the proposal to divide Canada into two provinces and the formation of a civil jurisdiction in Indian territory—the board's letters of June and August merely elaborated on the plans outlined in the hints.[5]

But if the proclamation merely stated formally and officially the hitherto unofficial and informal policy of the government, the ministry adhered to the proper methods for transacting interdepartmental business. These methods required the help of the board of trade. The plantation office was expected to translate *ad hoc* measures into official language suitable for a proclamation, a task requiring imagination as well as considerable experience of procedure. Subminister Maurice Morgann possessed the first trait, and John Pownall both.

The second of the two men, whose work was the most important, had served the board since 1741 and had been its secretary since 1758. Pownall, more than any other individual, turned the requests of the secretary of state in the spring to a proclamation of the Crown in the fall. His hand touched most of the official board proposals that finally went into the proclamation which included: no emigration from the older colonies to land

[5] Verner W. Crane, "Hints Relative to the Division of Government of the Conquered and Newly Acquired Countries in America," *Mississippi Valley Historical Review*, VIII (1921-1922), 367-373. Crane believes that Henry Ellis, former governor of Georgia and an old friend of William Knox, wrote the "hints." Knox himself asserted that Egremont received most of his colonial ideas from Ellis. Much of John Pownall's role in colonial policy has been outlined in Franklin B. Wickwire, "John Pownall and British Colonial Policy," *William and Mary Quarterly*, 3d ser., XX (1963), 543-554. The above section and other pages repeat many of the article's arguments, but more detail is given concerning Pownall's role in British-American trade relations following the Revolution.

beyond the Alleghenies; maintenance of a military force in the west; conciliar government in Canada; two-part division of Florida under royal government; encouragement of emigration to the Floridas; and regulation of the Indian trade.

Pownall particularly affected two of the recommendations. He drew up a "Sketch of a report concerning the cessions in Africa and America at the peace of 1763," which contained many of the ideas embodied in the board's report of June 8. The hints of Egremont included a plan for dividing Canada into two separate governments. Pownall disapproved the division, and it is perhaps significant that of the two clauses in the hints which the board of trade disapproved, that concerning the division of Canada was one. Many men had proposed different boundaries beyond which settlement should be forbidden, but the proclamation adopted the Appalachian range, the line suggested by Pownall.

During the summer of 1763 Lord Hillsborough replaced Shelburne at the board, and Lord Halifax became southern secretary. Although Halifax added some minor parts to the board report of August 5, these additions did not differ from decisions already reached, and a draft of the proclamation was ordered. Attorney General Yorke examined the draft, but Pownall reexamined it and altered it slightly, stressing the temporary policy of limiting western colonial expansion. Halifax approved the proclamation only after Pownall's reexamination and sent it to the council. Signed by the king, it became official colonial policy.[6]

Pownall had been at the very center of this work, although neither the secretary of state who opened the

[6] Humphreys, "Lord Shelburne," *E.H.R.*, XLIX (1934), 241-264, describes Pownall's work in detail.

correspondence with the board nor the head of the board during the initial stages of drafting remained in office for the entire period required for preparing the proclamation. Egremont died and Shelburne lost office before the proclamation was completed. Only Pownall participated from beginning to end with aid, advice and suggestions.

His colleague, Maurice Morgann, lightened the load during part of this period. Morgann, Shelburne's private secretary, held views which would have displeased many Americans. During the early stages of the proclamation's preparation Shelburne referred Morgann to Egremont's letter of May 5 and requested comments. Morgann complied with a document entitled "On American Commerce," which anticipated two later pieces of British legislation and reflected the prevailing mercantilist outlook of the government. "The British colonies are to be regarded in no other light," Morgann declared, "but as subservient to the commerce of their mother country. Colonists were merely factors for the purposes of trade, and in all considerations concerning the colonies, this must always be the leading idea." Morgann proposed revocation of all colonial charters in order to institute stronger control of America by the mother country. Charters gone, a tax should be levied on all colonial imports and exports except goods going to and from Britain or from one colony to another. Morgann wished this tax to support government officials and a military force in America. He proposed to eliminate colonial paper money, and thus anticipated the Parliamentary Act of 1764. He also wished to forbid colonial interior settlement in order to render the colonies "subservient to this kingdom" commercially. Only if the colonists remained close to the ocean could they export bulky goods and import European manufactures. The Crown, through the governor and other officers, should "exercise every act of sovereignty in each province" so that the colonies would be "relative and subservient to the commerce of Great Britain, which was the end of their establishment." Morgann further recommended the division of Canada and Florida into two different governments in each province.

Morgann also wrote, evidently later though still in connection with his work on the proclamation, "Plan for securing the future Dependence of the Provinces on the Continent of America." In this paper he fully endorsed the proposed line to limit colonial interior penetration, especially since closure of the western territory offered the mother country opportunities for closer colonial regulation. "That in the next place," he stated, "under pretence of regulating Indian trade, a very straight line be suddenly drawn on the back of the provinces and the country behind that line thrown, for the present, under the dominion of the Indians and the Indians be everywhere encouraged to support their own sovereignty." Military forces should be increased and stationed in East Florida, Nova Scotia, Canada, and in posts "the whole length of the navigation between Montreal and the mouths of the Mississippi, so that with the aid of a naval force, the whole of the provinces shall be surrounded." Encompassed by an army and hostile savages, limited in their finances, lacking proper leadership, the colonies could then be coerced into a due obedience to the mother country. Once absolutely obedient, the colonies would serve their proper role as factors for British commerce. The spirit, if not the substance of these proposals, was probably harsher than the spirit of any British legislation toward America before passage of the Boston Port Bill.[7]

The substance, if not the spirit, resembled Pownall's proposals, and Morgann, not Pownall, drafted the June 8 board report to Egremont that contained many of the ideas found in the proclamation. Both men had, however, offered similar propositions and both had participated in the preparation of the official report. The extent to which they influenced the final decisions of October defies precise statement. Plans, including Pownall's, had poured into the treasury long before the board of trade officially began work, and the proclamation only continued a policy begun several years previously. But both Pownall and Morgann participated vitally in the board's official administrative work.

Indeed, that work shows both sides of the subministerial coin—position and influence. Pownall's years of toil with the board, his knowledge of official procedure in colonial matters, resulting from long service as board secretary, endowed him with perhaps the largest share in the official preparation of the proclamation. But Morgann, with neither Pownall's experience nor his official status, also contributed importantly. His personal relationship with Lord Shelburne as the earl's private secretary evidently accounted for his participation. That relationship thrived through the 1760's and brought Morgann an undersecretaryship of state to Shelburne in the southern department in 1766. In this position he again worked on colonial problems, specifically the laws of Canada. Morgann, however, never enjoyed as did Pownall a continuous influence on policy. Like so many

[7] See Maurice Morgann, "On American Commerce," and "Plan for securing the future Dependence of the Provinces on the Continent of America," Shelburne Papers 85/26-34 and 67/107.

undersecretaries of state, his sporadic essays into government depended on the political fortunes of his superior.[8]

Pownall the official secretary and Morgann the private secretary contributed in only one of the three ways by which minor men influenced policy: they shaped into a precise proclamation the ministry's clearly outlined American proposals. Although such work involved them less in colonial affairs than did the other two avenues subministers sometimes followed, Pownall and Morgann definitely marked the Proclamation of 1763. Morgann would wander on and off the path of imperial decisions.[9] Pownall would continue straight down it.

---

[8] Morgann presents an interesting study in 1763 for his ideas toward America. Restrictive, unrealistic, bitterly hostile toward the colonies, Shelburne's secretary seemed to assume as early as 1763 that the colonies seriously contemplated immediate revolution and needed straightening. He assuredly did not gather these ideas from his chief. Whatever Shelburne's capabilities, and whether or not Shelburne had an American plan, he never seems to have been so openly hostile to America as his subordinate. Nor do the bits and scraps of information available on Morgann's life open any doors to understanding. His contemporaries knew more about his interests in the arts than in colonial problems. A powerful debater and a writer of note, Morgann wrung a rare admission from the famous lexicographer, Dr. Samuel Johnson. When the two men met at breakfast after a night-long dispute Johnson admitted: "Sir, I have been thinking on our dispute last night—*You were in the right.*" (Oxford edition of *Boswell's Life of Johnson* [Oxford, 1953], p. 1212). Morgann, of course, acquired yet greater notoriety with Shakespearian students for his brilliant *Essay on Falstaff*. Yet the versatile undersecretary may, perhaps, also be given credit for the improvement of the navy's system of signals, an achievement usually attributed to Captain Richard Kempenfelt. (See the very interesting letter from Maurice Morgann to Sir Joseph Banks, Mar. 3, 1789: B.M., MSS Add. 33,978, f. 231.) Able debater, Shakespearian scholar, friend of Dr. Johnson, Morgann had seemingly little reason for suspecting Americans of disloyalty to the Crown.

[9] Morgann joined the Chatham ministry as an undersecretary of

THE STAMP ACT

That path led Pownall a year after the proclamation into a new measure, the Stamp Act. Perhaps the single most important cause of the Revolution, the act's merits and demerits as well as its consequences have been debated endlessly. So have the character and aims of the man who assumed ultimate responsibility for it, First Lord of the Treasury George Grenville. This "prime minister" long suffered in the Whig histories of the Revolution. At worst he was a villain, and at best a cold man who perched himself in a "little watch tower" oblivious to colonial ferment.[10] Interested only in gaining a revenue, Grenville, according to the Whigs, spared little thought for the consequences of his policy.

The imperial historians of the twentieth century brushed some of the Whig tarnish from his reputation. C. W. Alvord, the first historian to examine at length British policy in the West, though not overly fond of the first lord, declared that

---

state to Shelburne in 1766 and again worked on colonial matters. He abstracted American papers for Charles Townshend and H. S. Conway, inquired into revenues raised in the West Indies, and composed a long opinion on the Massachusetts bill of indemnity and oblivion for those men who destroyed property in the Stamp Act riots. (See Shelburne Papers 57/243-245 and 58/243-248.) In 1767, through Shelburne's influence and by order of the privy council he was sent to Quebec to inquire into its laws and send back reports. (See Shortt and Doughty, *Canada Documents*, I, 199-200.) Morgann duly carried out his tasks, but again disappeared from the colonial scene to emerge once more in New York at the end of the Revolution as an aide to General Carleton helping clear loyalists claims there. His many letters in H.M.C., *American Manuscripts in the Royal Institution of Great Britain*, II (Dublin, 1906), III (Hereford, 1907), and IV (Hereford, 1909) show his importance to the general.

[10] See, for example, G. W. Greene, *Historical View of the American Revolution* (New York, 1876), pp. 52-53.

the Grenville-Bedford ministry should be credited with a serious attempt to solve the difficult and complex problem of the West; and whatever one's opinion of the results may be, it must be acknowledged that they had boldly faced the difficulties and had devised a comprehensive imperial program with provision for most of the possible exigencies.[11]

L. H. Gipson more recently termed Grenville the equal of Pitt in statesmanship and the superior of anyone in the understanding of financial matters.[12] Perhaps Charles R. Ritcheson praises the head of the treasury the most boldly. According to Ritcheson, Grenville "alone among British statesmen before the outbreak of the American Revolution offered a comprehensive plan which demonstrated true imperial statesmanship and a deep understanding of the British constitution."[13] Colonial Americans, of course, believed Grenville offered them little except taxes and tyranny.

Whatever the first lord of the treasury's understanding of the constitution, he unquestionably offered the colonies taxes. He held that Britain's financial solvency depended on finding new sources of revenue. Although British arms achieved victory in nearly every theater of operations during the Seven Years' War, the costs had been prodigious. Subsidies to the colonies, subsidies to European allies, payment of British troops in Germany and America, and supplies to British fleets from the Mediterranean to the Indian Ocean had burdened the nation heavily. The treasury had managed to finance

[11] Alvord, *Mississippi Valley*, I, 224.

[12] Lawrence H. Gipson, *The Coming of the Revolution, 1763-1775* (New York, 1954), p. 57.

[13] Charles R. Ritcheson, *British Politics and the American Revolution* (Norman, Okla., 1954), p. 9.

the war, but the resultant national debt seemed to contemporaries to be enormous. According to L. H. Gipson, "despite unprecedented wartime taxation, with the supply bills from 1756 to the end of 1766 reaching an annual average of some £14,500,000 or a total of over £145,000,000, the debt at the end of this decade was still over £133,000,000."[14] Thus "financial conditions in England at this time," Dora Mae Clark states, "gave some cause for alarm and inspired a sense of urgency in the quest for revenue."[15] Since the war had in part been fought to save the American colonies from French domination, Grenville failed to see why the colonies should not share the cost of maintaining British troops on their frontiers for future protection against Indians and a possible French resurgence. He only questioned the best way to secure this revenue, and his ministry thought it found an answer in the Stamp Act. Yet Grenville, despite his ultimate responsibility, personally deserves no more credit, or discredit, for the specific measure than his subordinates. The Grenville ministry involved much more than the wishes or actions of its head.

Indeed the first lord needed, as much or more than any other minister, subministerial help with American problems. He was assuredly a past master at British finance—few doubted it. He proved an able politician and a strong prime minister during the Wilkes crisis. He possessed an unusual ability for attracting able and industrious men. Yet his correspondence scarcely reveals that he thought deeply about, much less understood, American problems. He lacked great imagination. As John Brooke noted, Grenville held a "completely logical policy

14 Gipson, *Coming of the Revolution*, pp. 55-56. Note the great increase from 1755, when the national debt stood at £75,000,000.

15 Clark, *British Treasury*, p. 116.

towards America. . . . He held that America could be taxed and ought to be taxed, and he repeated it over and over again *ad nauseam.*"[16]

This unoriginal view did not necessarily propel the prime minister into the details necessary for its realization. Knowing little of America, he had to rely upon subordinates for all the information necessary to an American bill. He might approve or reject their work. If he found it satisfactory he had the energy to push the results of that work through Parliament, but the surest mark of that ability was his use of imaginative and able subministers. Indeed, the Stamp Act bore in two ways an even greater subministerial impress than did the Proclamation of 1763. In the first place, although the statute originated in the treasury, neither Grenville nor his staff there possessed the information necessary to compile legislation of its scope. The treasury necessarily called upon the minor men in other departments, and the talents of several subministers finally contributed to the basic wording of the Stamp Act. Secondly, and seemingly paradoxically, one subminister, Grenville's treasury secretary, Thomas Whately, was more responsible for the measure than any one subminister had been for the proclamation. To Whately fell the task of gathering data from his colleagues in Britain and his friends in the colonies. He further coordinated the several preparations of the act and supervised its final drafting. His work in the end exemplified the second of the three ways subministers affected policy—shaping general ministerial intentions into a specific statute.

Whately owed his political career to Grenville, which probably accounts for much of his zeal for his chief's

[16] Brooke, *Chatham Administration,* pp. 98-99.

American plans. Whately attended Cambridge and the Middle Temple and was admitted to the bar, but through Grenville's "favour" abandoned the law and entered the treasury in August of 1763. He soon came to share the first lord's belief in the necessity for British financial solvency. He knew, as did Grenville, that forcing the colonies to pay for the British troops protecting their frontiers and the administration of Indian affairs would draw Britain closer to this goal. Whately further believed, as did most Englishmen, in parliamentary supremacy. He naturally supported measures which he thought best suited his superior's and Britain's requirements. No man so attached to the Grenville party could do less, and his legal mind must have joyed to serve a minister who hoped for a system of clearly defined imperial relationships and well-ordered finances.

If Whately approached American problems with certain fixed and unalterable attitudes, he was nonetheless as well suited to supervise construction of a stamp act as many of the other men connected with the treasury. His absolute loyalty to his chief guaranteed assiduous attention to the project, more attention than might be expected from his secretarial colleague, Charles Jenkinson. The latter, a protégé of Lord Bute, helped Whately but did not accord to the operation the same concentration. The man whom Grenville "favoured," furthermore, professed an "inclination" for colonial administration and claimed that he "always loved the Colonies." He probably did, for he had taken the trouble, even before becoming secretary, to cultivate several men who were, or later became, prominent Americans. Foremost among them were John Temple of Boston, surveyor general of customs in the northern part of America; Jared Ingersoll, the Connecticut merchant who became

law proceedings would be stamped? Were cards and dice stamped? How many newspapers did Massachusetts have? How much money did Temple think the Stamp Act would produce?

In appraising responses to these queries Whately faced his first administrative difficulties. Neither Ingersoll nor Temple favored a stamp act. Ingersoll told the secretary that not only did Connecticut resent strongly an American stamp measure, but the neighboring provinces were "filled with the most dreadfull apprehensions from such a step's taking place."[19] Temple deemed the proposed Stamp Act neither "expedient" nor "prudent."[20] A dilemma confronted the treasury secretary: he had to draft an act for America against American wishes. Whately surmounted the obstacle by pretending that it did not exist. He would "not give entire credit to all the objections that are raised on your side of the water." "I doubt that they [the colonists] are inclined to object to all taxes," he asserted, "and yet some are absolutely necessary." Unless "unforeseen objections" occurred, the Stamp Act would probably be extended to America in 1765. Whately stepped irreversibly toward the legislation.[21]

The less hostile advice of royal officials, other boards, and subministers hastened the steps. Lord Halifax, Egremont's successor as secretary of state, asked colonial governors to describe the papers used in courts of law. Their answers would help determine what papers to stamp.[22]

[19] Jared Ingersoll to Thomas Whately, July 6, 1764: *Ingersoll Papers*, pp. 295-301.

[20] John Temple to Thomas Whately, Sept. 10, 1764: *Bowdoin and Temple Papers*, pp. 24-25.

[21] Thomas Whately to John Temple, Aug. 14 and Nov. 5, 1764: *Ibid.*, 22-23, 37.

[22] P.R.O., T. 1/430, contains the answers of Governors Wentworth, Franklin, and Deputy Governor Wright of Pennsylvania.

Charles Jenkinson corresponded with the secretary to the English stamp commissioners in order to ascertain the difference between Scottish and English stamp duties.[23] John Pownall furnished documents concerning a former proposal to tax New York in 1710 that could be used as a precedent for the new scheme.[24] The outline of a mysterious "Mr. X" proved vastly important. In 1763 the ministry hired a lawyer to work out the details of a stamp bill for America. He presented a plan for a stamp act which it approved in preference to another submitted by Henry McCulloh, the colonial speculator. The British Museum houses a paper listing X's expenses, the persons consulted, and the documents examined. Unfortunately X failed to sign his name, although the legal terminology he used to describe sessions of the year—Hilary term, for example—attests to his being a lawyer. The results of all this work by Halifax, Jenkinson, Pownall, and others arrived sooner or later on Whately's desk. Even X labored closely under Whately's supervision, copying documents, consulting precedents, pouring over manuscripts, and frequenting the premises of the plantation office. He contributed greatly to the text of the Stamp Act itself,[25] but his information went along with much

[23] See John Brettell, secretary to the stamp board, to Charles Jenkinson, Dec. 18, 1764: B.M., MSS Add. 38,203, f. 314.

[24] John Pownall to Charles Jenkinson, Dec. 26, 1764: B.M., MSS Add. 38,203, f. 328.

[25] Charles R. Ritcheson, "The Preparation of the Stamp Act," *William and Mary Quarterly*, 3d ser., x (1953), 543-559, detailed the work of Mr. X, but mistakenly identified him as John Tabor Kempe, attorney general for New York. It is possible that Thomas Augustus Cruwys, the solicitor to the stamp office, was Mr. X. At least Henry McCulloh's statement of his objection to the Stamp Act includes the following: "I was desired to Assist Mr. Cruwys in drawing the Stamp Duty Bill." See Jack P. Greene, " 'A Dress of Horror!' Henry McCulloh's Objections to the Stamp Act," *Hunting-*

other material into a draft that Whately finally completed for the treasury.

He presented that draft in the last month of 1764.
The men who read and approved it on December 7
openly acknowledged its author, for it was entitled "Mr.
Whately's plan of a Stamp Act for the colonies & plantations." The secretary's tasks, however, had only begun.
Transforming the draft into an act of Parliament and
working out the several details for its administration ex-
acted as much from Whately and his colleagues as the initial preparation itself had. Indeed, perhaps nothing measures better the subministerial impact on the Stamp Act
than their work after the treasury had accepted Whately's outline.

At least from an administrative point of view it was
a complex document whose several wrinkles required
pressing by firm administrative irons. For example, although the second paragraph noted that a bill referring
to the power of commissioners, the penalties for offenses against the act, and clauses for the prevention of
fraud and evasion had already been drawn, the "rates,
and the mode of distribution" were still unsettled. The
plan also designated materials to be stamped, but its
suggested method of remittance was not followed. Whately had intended that the stamp commissioners furnish
the paymaster general with bills upon their head distributor. The latter would pay the commissioners the value
of such bills, which the commissioners would in turn pay
into the exchequer.[26]

---

ton Library Quarterly, xxvi (1963), 253-262. Yet McCulloh admits
the ministry rejected his plans, and if they were the same as those
he concerted in conjunction with Cruwys, then X must have been
someone other than Cruwys. X's account of his work is in B.M.,
MSS Add. 35,911, ff. 18-36.

[26] See "Mr. Whately's plan of a stamp act for the colonies &
plantations," B.M., MSS Add. 35,910, ff. 310-323.

But this scheme failed of adoption. In April Jenkinson proposed an alternate, stating that he had "settled a plan for remitting the American revenue."[27] Twelve days later the treasury read yet another suggestion for the same purpose, which involved an arrangement between the agents of those contractors who paid the troops in the colonies and the custom's collectors. The treasury ordered the customs informed of this plan which, the lords hoped, would "prevent as much as possible, the inconveniences and difficulties of bringing money out of the colonies in America, and the West Indies." If the revenue commissioners found no objections they could order their American collectors to pay Stamp Act revenue to the contractors' agents. The collector, in turn, would take from the agents bills upon the agents' principals in London. These bills would be payable to the receiver general of the customs.[28] Yet this scheme, like all the previous ones, never secured a final approval. In July, long after Whately's original "plan" had been accepted and the Stamp Act had become law, the treasury had still not settled a method for payment of troops without bringing money to England. The lords commissioners failed to arrive at a final solution until July 9. On that day they at last decided that all money arising from the Stamp Act should be paid to the deputy postmaster in America, or whomever he authorized to receive it, so that the duties could at all times be applied "to defray the subsistence of the troops and any military expenses incurred in the colonies." The lords ordered that the deputy postmaster in America receive sums held by the customs collectors or stamp distributors and in return give them bills on the postmaster general. Such bills would be

[27] Charles Jenkinson to George Grenville, Apr. 13, 1765: Murray—Grenville Papers, file B 2, Jenkinson folder.
[28] P.R.O., T. 29/36, pp. 323-324, minute of Apr. 26, 1765.

payable to the receiver general of the customhouse or stamp office, while the money, applied to the payment of troops, would be accounted for by the deputy postmaster.[29] Thus with Whately's plan already approved, with the Stamp Act already law, the subministers—treasury secretaries and customs commissioners—worked as late as July of 1765 to devise the method for paying troops the money the act hoped to raise.

Subministers also worked out, after the bill became an act, the number, duties, and pay of various personnel to be connected with the stamp duty. Whately's "plan" had suggested salaried American inspectors, allowed ample travel money, to check on the revenue officers. It had also proposed that 1s. 6d. in the pound go to the head stamp distributor and 1s. in the pound to the under distributor. The English stamp office would, of course, incur additional expense: increased salaries would go to some personnel, and new officers would also have to be appointed. The stamp board accepted this basic plan, but it continued to dicker with the treasury secretary. In April the commissioners proposed an expanded and slightly different scheme. The distributors should receive eight per cent of the money collected, from which they would pay themselves, their servants, and the under distributors and should further enjoy free postage of letters, carriage of goods, and returns of monies. The stamp board further requested £100 a year and 20s. a day travel money for inspectors. The secretary to the English stamp board, the receiver general, and the receiver general's first clerk all merited increased salaries, the commissioners argued, and the comptroller needed an additional clerk at £50 a year. They further suggested a set of chambers for a warehouse to store American stamps, the necessary ware-

[29] P.R.O., T. 29/37, f. 31, minute of July 9, 1765.

house keeper, a warehouse officer to pack goods consigned to the stamp distributors, and a chamber-keeper at an extra £10 a year.[30] On July 5 the treasury approved the stamp commissioners' plan.[31] Together with Whately the stamp board had arrived at one of the most vital features in the administration of the act, the payment of personnel involved in it.

Before these men could be paid, however, they had to be appointed and supplied with the necessary stamps. Again, subministers arranged the details. After the act became law, the stamp office necessarily apportioned the stamps between America and the West Indies and found the proper securities for each province.[32] But they had to leave to the treasury the appointment of men to distribute the stamps. Grenville evidently took little interest in this part of his patronage, for many officers had not been assigned by April. He may have permitted Whately some decisions, for he had allowed his subordinate to share in North American customs appointments. Contemporaries, at any rate, believed Whately could hasten the arrangements if not make them himself, and John Bretell, secretary to the stamp office, reminded him of his duty in April. "Time advances," Brettell said, "and we have but few officers appointed in America. You will please to recollect, we are to write to those distributors that are now resident there, to propose their securities, then to send over their bonds to be executed and to wait 'till that is returned before any stamps can be sent."[33]

30 Stamp commissioners to the treasury, Apr. 27, 1765: P.R.O., T. 1/439, ff. 79-80.

31 P.R.O., T. 29/37, ff. 29-30, minute of July 5, 1765.

32 John Brettell to Charles Jenkinson, Mar. 26, 1765: B.M., MSS Add. 38,204, f. 166.

33 John Bretell to Thomas Whately, Apr. 25, 1765: P.R.O., T.

Appointment of collectors, apportioning of stamps, paying American officers, and many more details required the firm touch of Whately and other subministers. Vital administrative duties, they carried little glamor and rarely attracted the talents of cabinet ministers. Yet the great politicians could never have envisaged a Stamp Act had the subministers not been present to give it form and substance. More than any others, the minor men stayed with the statute administratively from its tentative beginnings in England to its riotous and bloody end in North America. No one person originated the measure. Indeed, the notion of a Stamp Act for America had revolved in ministerial circles long before George Grenville took the seals of treasury office.[34] Grenville had

---

1/439, ff. 57-58. Although all these cooperative endeavors were necessary to the administrative implementation of the Stamp Act, they came after the basic plan had been accepted. Many vital administrative considerations—number, duties, pay of personnel connected with the act, apportionment of stamps between America and the West Indies, appointment of American officers—had not even been completed by the time the stamp bill became the Stamp Act. Considerable confusion surrounds the Stamp Act. Indeed, perhaps the most important cause of the Revolution lies under an administrative cloud. See App. B.

[34] Of course a stamp duty had been in effect in England for many years. See Edward Hughes, "English Stamp Duties, 1664-1764," *E.H.R.*, LVI (1941), 234-259. One of the more interesting early proposals for an American stamp duty is found in the Monson Papers 25/2/82, Lincoln Record Office. Although undated and unsigned the document was written shortly after Gov. Shirley took office in Massachusetts. The author proposed a stringent enforcement of laws designed to preserve the king's woods in America, and that in all future land grants quit rents should go to the king. He urged that New Englanders be forbidden to manufacture iron and that the drawback granted Americans on all items exported from England be removed. Finally he asserted: "If stampt papers extended to the plantations, a vast revenue would arise from it. In New England the people are very litigious so they would use many

the courage of his convictions and proposed that his ministry tax America, but Thomas Whately worked out the means to do it. In the process he called upon the talents of Mr. X, Jared Ingersoll, John Temple, various colonial governors, and a host of subministers. Grenville, as the responsible minister, approved the work and steered it through Parliament, but did little else. Multiple subministerial efforts helped Thomas Whately turn the general policy of taxation into a specific, and highly consequential, Stamp Act.[35]

THE SUGAR ACT

A second highly consequential statute, the Sugar Act, also emerged from the Grenville ministry. It never excited as much immediate controversy because it related to imperial trade, yet it intended, as much as the Stamp Act, to tax Americans. Since it succeeded where its fellow "internal" revenue attempt failed, the Sugar Act assuredly deserves to stand among the major causes of the American Revolution. The subministers again also deserve added posture, for they created it. If Thomas Whately and his colleagues breathed life into the Grenville ministry's stamp proposals, another set of subministers, the customs commissioners, shaped its ideas about sugar. Indeed, the customs board fulfilled the third and most important subministerial function in American colonial policy: it actually suggested an imperial measure the British government adopted. The Sugar Act—a creature of the revenue commissioners—would alter consider-

---

stamps. Why should they who pay no quitt rents or taxes to ye crown be on a better footing than his Majesty's subject in England?"

[35] Although the Stamp Act was Whately's major contribution to policy, a portion of his letters, read publicly to the Massachusetts Assembly after his death, excited ill will between the Bay Colony and Britain. See App. A.

ably the customs system in the commerce between Britain and America.

A general tightening of this system and an enforced collection of all legal monies due the Crown, Grenville hoped, would add considerably to the revenue. When he first entered office he essayed, with the aid of Treasury Secretary Whately, to stop publishers from evading the English stamp duties. He sought a more efficient method of collecting the land tax and salt duties and curbed extraordinary expenditures in the army. He tried to halt the illicit trade between England and the continental nations and even required English consuls abroad to report on this trade. He repeatedly attempted to wipe out smuggling in Jersey and Guernsey and cleaned out what hitherto had been a perpetual nest of smugglers through government purchase, and hence government control, of the Isle of Man. Yet though all these measures decreased British debts, they did not substantially help to make America pay for itself. Grenville only skirted the main problem, the continental colonies, by stationing schooners in the St. Lawrence to prevent Canadian smuggling and selling lands in the West Indies for a quick revenue.[36] He faced the issue squarely with his internal tax, the Stamp Act, but he leaned heavily on the customs board for the right path to follow in taxing trade. The board speeded him along toward the Sugar Act.

It has been argued that the origins of this measure

[36] For these activities, see P.R.O., T. 1/422, ff. 47-58; Philip Stephens to Charles Jenkinson, July 10, 1764: P.R.O., T. 1/434, ff. 270-274; "An extract of letters from his majesty's consuls abroad, relative to the illicit trade, carried on between his majesty's dominions and the several countries wherein they respectively reside," Oct. 16, 1764: P.R.O., T. 1/429, ff. 301-303; P.R.O., T. 29/35 and T. 29/36, pp. 364, 188, minutes of Apr. 14, 1764, and Dec. 11, 1764; and collectors of salt duties to the treasury, Oct. 31, 1764: P.R.O., T. 1/434, ff. 82-87.

lay in a representation by Henry McCulloh to the British government in 1761. McCulloh's proposals supposedly accounted for the substantive ideas the customs board submitted to the treasury in a report of September 16, 1763. This report, in turn, outlined the future Sugar Act and needed only the drafting of its proposals into a parliamentary bill to become official policy.[37]

This account of the origins, however, credits McCulloh with too much and the customs commissioners with too little. The latter, in fact, propounded measures similar to those found in the Sugar Act two years before McCulloh's representation and four years before Grenville took office. On May 10, 1759, the commissioners wrote to the treasury upon receipt of a letter from John Pownall. Pownall had sent them "several letters & representations" concerning illegal colonial trade and "improper practices which have been set up" to defy the Navigation Acts. The commissioners proposed to remedy these

[37] John C. Miller, *Origins of the American Revolution* (Boston, 1943), p. 100, credited McCulloh with the original proposal, and Allen S. Johnson, "The Passage of the Sugar Act," *William and Mary Quarterly*, 3d ser., XVI (1959), 507-514, also accepts McCulloh. Greene, "McCulloh's Objections," *Huntington Library Quarterly*, XXVI (1963), 253-262, in his introduction to McCulloh's protests shows how McCulloh had earlier been given credit for proposing measures, in this case the Stamp Act, which had in fact been discussed long before McCulloh's presentations. Since completion of this manuscript, Thomas G. Barrow, "Background to the Grenville Program, 1757-1763," *William and Mary Quarterly*, 3d ser., XXII (1965), 93-104, has outlined in detail the origins of the Sugar Act. Barrow credits the customs commissioners with the proposal in 1759 to the ministry that Grenville's administration later incorporated into the Sugar Act. Barrow, however, notes that the board of trade first urged the customs to action, on the basis of the board's information about violations of the Navigation Acts. Although Barrow thus carries the origins of the Sugar Act back further than 1759, his conclusions about the influence of the customs commissioners on the measure are similar to my own.

abuses. They entered into few details but considered three main points: (1) the illegal importation of rum and molasses from the French West Indies into the New England colonies; (2) the importation of European goods into North America and the carrying of enumerated goods thence to Europe contrary to the Navigation Acts; and (3) the "pernicious practice" of supplying the French in the Caribbean with goods either from the American colonies or from Ireland. The commissioners hoped to end all three practices. First, they would lower the duty on molasses. "So long as the high duty on foreign rum, sugar & molasses imposed by the act of the 6th of his present Majesty, & then intended we apprehend as a prohibition, continues," they argued, "the running of these goods into his Majt.'s northern colonies will be unavoidable." Second, they wished to impose stricter warrants for good behavior on the merchants or their agents, for they considered present bonds and cockets insufficiently binding. They also noted that smuggling cases put in suit were handled in ordinary colonial courts, "where it is apprehended that verdicts upon points of this nature are not so impartial as in England." This statement implied, of course, that a stricter court—one without prejudiced juries—ought to try violations of the trade laws. Only the vice-admiralty court, among the colonial courts, dispensed with juries. Third, the commissioners requested help to enforce revenue laws. They considered the limited number of revenue officers insufficient to cope with the problem. The only other organization which could offer help was the British navy.[38]

No immediate parliamentary legislation ensued along

[38] Commissioners of customs to treasury, May 10, 1759: P.R.O., T. 1/430, ff. 351-353.

the lines recommended, undoubtedly because the Seven Years' War required efforts elsewhere. During that war, however, the British navy had been authorized to seize vessels trading with the enemy and, according to Carl Ubbelohde, had been "surprisingly successful in tracking down violations." Parliamentary statute enlarged upon these powers after the conclusion of peace. After May 1, 1763, naval officers, sworn as customs officials, "could seize and prosecute violations of the acts of trade" and secure as a reward a share of the condemned cargoes.[39]

Implementation of the new statute required executive action, and it only answered part of George Grenville's needs. While ministerial orders might help prevent smuggling, they could not raise a revenue. Yet the treasury needed to look no farther than the year-old outline of the customs commissioners for a satisfactory plan. Although the report of 1759, unlike the Sugar Act of 1764, intended only to stop smuggling and not raise a revenue, its essential features found their way into the Sugar Act.

That act properly began when Whately's colleague at the treasury, Charles Jenkinson, wrote to the customs commissioners in May by treasury order, asking for their suggestions on how to increase American customs revenue. They had not responded by July 20, so Jenkinson exhorted them to hurry. His prodding resulted next day in the first of two reports by the commissioners which, added to the one of 1759, provided the basis for the Sugar Act. The board restated its belief in the necessity for reducing the high duties on foreign sugar, rum, and molasses. It did not detail the method of "condemning seizures in the courts of admiralty and not by juries," but

[39] Carle Ubbelohde, *The Vice-Admiralty Courts and the American Revolution* (Chapel Hill, 1960), pp. 38-39. The statute is 3 Geo. III, c. 22.

such a legal procedure would obviously conform to the hopes expressed earlier. The commissioners further considered it absolutely necessary to compel customs officers in America to maintain a "constant residence at their stations." Too many officers absented themselves by unnecessary journeys. Those men who worked conscientiously, however, could only execute revenue laws with the full aid and cooperation of civil and military officials. Finally, the commissioners noted that if revenue officers in America were deprived of fees and allowed instead poundage out of their remittances, their profits would "keep pace only with their diligence."[40]

The treasury lords immediately read the report. They noted that the provisions regarding fees and lowering of duty could be effected only by parliamentary enactment, but that American customs officers could be ordered immediately to reside in America. The customs should at once command all officers to duty at their stations and require from them a strict accounting and a constant correspondence with the treasury specifying their proceedings and suggested improvements. Jenkinson requested the customs board to carry out these decisions, and orders went into effect. Laxity had ended. Revenue officers who failed to obey the new orders faced loss of position. The ministry had stepped firmly toward tighter customs collection in America, and if the treasury had authorized the procedure, the recommendation had come from the commissioners of customs. Indeed, Grenville himself acknowledged the board initiative in a letter to Horace Walpole.[41]

[40] Charles Jenkinson to customs commissioners, May 21 and July 20, 1763: P.R.O., T. 11/27, pp. 283, 303, and commissioners of customs to treasury, July 21, 1763: P.R.O., T. 1/426, ff. 269-272.

[41] Horace Walpole pleaded with Grenville to retain a Philadelphia customs collector since the officer had been appointed by Sir

Grenville's treasury also complied with a second proposal of the commissioners, initially made in 1759 and repeated in 1763, that civil and military officers in America support customs officers. Egremont, secretary of state for the southern department, vested naval commanders in the colonies with the "necessary and legal powers, from the commissioners of the customs" to help revenue officers catch smugglers. Egremont also commanded all colonial governors to cooperate in the suppression of smuggling. The treasury ordered copies of his letter sent to all American revenue officers, "for their encouragement in the discharge of their duty, and that they may know in cases of difficulty where to have recourse." Soon ships of the British navy supplemented revenue cutters in the twofold task of stopping smuggling and raising a revenue. Any naval commander could now ask for, and secure, deputations for himself and his officers to act as revenue officers in the colonies if the commander's orders sent him to America.[42] "Even though

---

Robert Walpole and had held office for twenty-five years. Grenville replied that he had nothing against the collector, but that the customs had stated that the revenue would be improved if officers stopped farming their positions, resided in America, and tended to their work. Grenville saw no alternatives. Walpole's friend must either go to America or lose his position. See George Grenville to Horace Walpole, Sept. 8, 1763: *Grenville Papers*, II, 114.

[42] To procure deputations the admiralty secretary wrote to the customs and named the ship going to America. He then requested deputations for the captain and those officers whom the captain chose. See for example Philip Stephens to William Wood, Aug. 20, 1763: P.R.O., Adm. 2/536, p. 233. The naval officers, who took a share of the seizures, sometimes found themselves hindered by resentful or lazy customs officers and on other occasions helped from difficulties by those very people the navy was supposed to help. For instance, Captain Bishop, commander of a sloop stationed off Boston, seized a vessel from Bordeaux carrying on illicit trade. He

officers of his Majesty's ships-of-war felt that hunting for
smugglers was beneath their dignity," Dora Mae Clark
avers, "in succeeding years they made a major contribution to the unusual number of seizures, and consequently, to the revenue."[43]

Executive authority increased naval support and tight-
ened customs regulations, but the treasury needed more
specific information before putting any bills to Parliament. Late in July the treasury lords asked the revenue
commissioners what "further checks and restraints"
could be imposed in America and requested a better
method of condemning seizures "& distributing the money
arising therefrom."[44] In September the revenue board

---

seized it and at the same time complained that the customs officials
neglected their duty. See Philip Stephens to Charles Jenkinson,
Dec. 21, 1763: P.R.O., T. 1/424, f. 707. The treasury, of course,
ordered the customs board to inquire into the conduct of lax American officers and command those officers to support Captain Bishop
in the prosecution of his suit and condemnation of the seized vessel.
See P.R.O., T. 29/35, p. 251, minute of Jan. 9, 1764. On another
occasion Captain Browne of the sloop *Hawke* was shoved into jail
in New York on the suit of the owner of a ship which Browne had
seized on the advice of the attorney general of New York. Browne
lost his case in court. The customs board immediately ordered the
collector and comptroller of New York to find bail for Browne. The
commissioners also noted to John Temple, surveyor general of customs in northern America, that like cases could happen in the
future. If naval officers made legal seizures and yet were prosecuted,
the commissioners authorized Temple to order collectors and comptrollers to enter into bail for imprisoned officers. The board added:
"You must repeat our directions to the officers of the several ports
within your district; that they aid and assist the officers of the navy,
acting in their duty as officers of the revenue, to the utmost of their
power." Thus the colonial situation demanded not only naval aid
to customs, but customs aid to the navy to get the latter's officers out
of jail.

[43] Clark, *British Treasury*, p. 134.

[44] P.R.O., T. 29/35, pp. 135-136, minute of July 29, 1763.

elaborated upon their previous outlines and furnished nearly all the details necessary for the Sugar Act of 1764. The commissioners suggested lowering the duty on sugar, rum, and molasses; a more extensive and more complicated system of bonds and cockets so that shipmasters could not easily evade the provisions of their sworn depositions; payment of all monetary forfeitures and penalties in sterling instead of colonial currency; and establishment of a colonial judicature to try customs violations "in so precise a manner, and under the decision of such proper persons, that justice may in all cases of this sort be diligently and impartially administer'd."[45] The treasury read and approved this report, sent the entire customs plan to the king, and directed the commissioners to prepare the "draught of a bill to be presented to Parliament" in accordance with the recommendations.[46]

The revenue board and its staff carried out this directive in conjunction with the treasury secretaries. Many specific details—facts, figures, revenue gains on specific items, exact wording of legislation—still demanded consideration. Commissioner Edward Hooper, according to Richard Jackson, collected material on "some American subjects respecting the customs" in the summer of 1763, during the period when he helped prepare the customs report of September.[47] William Wood, the cus-

[45] Customs commissioners to treasury lords, Sept. 16, 1763: P.R.O., T. 1/462, ff. 289-291.

[46] Treasury to customs commissioners, Sept. 21, 1763: P.R.O., T. 29/35, p. 164; Thomas Whately to customs commissioners, Sept. 21, 1763: P.R.O., T. 11/27, pp. 319-320; and P.R.O., T. 29/35, pp. 168-173, minute of Sept. 28, 1763. By late December the draft seems to have been completed. At that time one of the four principal clerks of the treasury had noted that he had just finished the bill in conjunction with the solicitor to the customs. See Robert Yeates to Charles Jenkinson, Dec. 29, 1763: *Jenkinson Papers*, p. 245.

[47] Richard Jackson to Charles Jenkinson, Sept. 18, 1763: *Jenkinson Papers*, pp. 191-192.

toms secretary, sent Treasury Secretary Jenkinson accounts of enumerated duties from the year 1710 and an account of the duties of 6 George II. He also gave the treasury secretary a notation of money paid into the exchequer by the receiver general for the past three years.[48] John Freemantle, senior clerk at the customs, former plantation clerk and future customs secretary, also furnished information to Jenkinson. Freemantle sent an account of the net produce of duties on the Molasses Act.[49] These accounts and other material prompted Treasury Secretary Whately to recommend a tax of 3*d.* on the gallon for imported foreign molasses, a figure accepted by the treasury.[50]

One subsidiary detail, an indirect tax on America, may also have been worked out by the subministers at this time. This section of the Sugar Act, in itself an important departure from policy, denied to Americans the drawbacks they had formerly enjoyed. Perhaps Commissioner Musgrave added this proviso to the act. He was the first, and seemingly the only, official to recognize its significance some twenty years later when the ministry, after losing the war, tried to patch its trade relations with the now-independent United States. In 1783 Musgrave bellicosely told William Eden: "Till the act of the 4th of Geo. 3 Chap. 15 which gives the Americans

[48] See William Wood to Charles Jenkinson, Jan. 9 and Jan. 10, 1764, and Charles Jenkinson to William Wood, Jan. 9, 1764: *Jenkinson Papers*, pp. 252-254. Four days earlier, Wood had informed his colleague of the method of receiving and accounting American duties. See P.R.O., T. 11/27, p. 372. Jucker does not publish the accounts of enumerated duties, but they may be found in B.M., MSS Add. 38,334, f. 221.

[49] John Freemantle to Charles Jenkinson, Jan. 31, 1764: B.M., MSS Add. 38,202, f. 71.

[50] Johnson, "Passage of the Sugar Act," *William and Mary Quarterly*, 3d ser., XVI (1959), 511-512.

less drawbacks than the rest of the world is repealed, England is exactly like a shopkeeper who showed over his door that he will make all customers whose Christian names are William pay five pct. more than any others."[51] The commissioner referred not to the lowering of duty on sugar, rum, and molasses, the main features of the Sugar Act, but to paragraph xiii, which stipulated that after May 1, 1764,

> . . . no part of the rate or duty, commonly called *The Old Subsidy*, shall, be repaid or drawn back for any foreign goods the growth, production, or manufacture, of *Europe*, or of the *East Indies*, which shall be exported from this kingdom to any *British* colony or plantation in *America* (wines, white callicoes, and muslins only excepted) any law, custom, or usage, to the contrary notwithstanding.

Paragraph xvi put teeth in xiii. Any merchant who entered goods for export, claimed such goods were not America bound in order to obtain a drawback, and then shipped them there anyway forfeited the drawback. The exporter and the master of the ship, furthermore, forfeited double the amount of the drawback and treble the amount of the goods. America would thus provide an indirect revenue because Britain could save the money formerly spent on colonial rebates. American merchants would now, in theory, have to land European products in England before reshipment to America, pay the required duty, and then receive no compensation for their time and trouble. If carried into effect these provisions should have raised considerably the price of non-English

---

[51] Musgrave believed these provisions were passed "indirectly to raise a revenue from the plantations." See Sir William Musgrave to William Eden, Mar. 10, 1783: B.M., MSS Add. 34.419, f. 120.

goods sent to America. Whether or not Musgrave spon-
sored this unique feature, it departed in no way from the
general policies enunciated by the customs commissioners. Along with several other paragraphs it appeared
in statute form when George III signed the Sugar Bill
into an act as 4 George III c. 15.

This measure realized one of the revenue board's
recommendations of 1759 and 1763. The executive action
that sent customs officers to their duties in North America
and furnished them naval assistance completed the second
of its proposals. Only broadening of the admiralty's legal
jurisdiction in America remained to finish the trio. The
ministry moved toward this end during construction of
the Sugar Act.

Vice-admiralty courts, of course, had long existed
in North America. In each colony such a body could
try offenses against the Navigation Acts. But the provincial vice-admiralty courts, according to Carl Ubbelohde, suffered from three impediments to effective action: (1) the judges, appointed by the provincial governors, were so partial to the merchants that suits brought
by customs officers fared badly; (2) the colonists' attempts
to use the common-law courts to negate or supersede
admiralty jurisdiction, even if unsuccessful, so confused
and muddled issues as to render satisfactory decisions
difficult; and (3) "the jurisdiction of the provincial vice-
admiralty courts had always been limited to cases arising
within the borders of their own province. A seizure in
Pennsylvania had to be tried in a Pennsylvania court,
regardless of the residence of the ship's owners, or the
place of its registry."[52] What was needed and what
the customs commissioners obviously expected, was a

[52] Ubbelohde, *Vice-Admiralty Courts*, p. 49.

single, powerful court not open to merchant influence and unrestricted in its jurisdiction.

The creation of such a "supercourt" necessitated extensive preparation. In pursuance of the treasury's recommendations the admiralty lords met in October of 1763 to consider a uniform plan for admiralty courts in North America. They first secured the opinions of the attorney and solicitor generals on the legal questions involved in the plan. Did the admiralty have power to appoint a vice-admiral for all North America with his attendant judge and officers? If so, could the vice-admiralties already established still exercise their respective jurisdictions in their respective provinces? Would the new court have cognizance in cases where "forfeitures and penalties are incurred by virtue of any of the acts of Parliament which seem to confine the jurisdiction locally to the courts of vice-admiralty, or common law, within each respective province."[53] All major questions seemed answered by the spring of 1764, when the crown lawyers approved establishment of a court for all North America, and the admiralty decided to appoint a judge resident there at a salary of £800 a year. The admiralty then proposed to the council, with treasury approval, that the judge of vice-admiralty be paid out of seizures of prohibited and uncustomed goods. If such funds proved insufficient, he could supplement them with profits from the sale of unserviceable naval stores. An order in council of April 18 followed the admiralty proposals and appointed a vice-admiralty judge for all North America, resident in Halifax.[54] This directive complet-

[53] P.R.O., Adm. 3/71, minute of Oct. 19, 1763.
[54] P.R.O., T. 1/429, ff. 156-159, and T. 29/35, p. 355, minute of April 6, 1764. It should be pointed out, however, that the new court enjoyed no more than concurrent jurisdiction with the pro-

ed the recommendations of the English customs board. A group of subministers had proposed, and in good part implemented, another disastrously consequential piece of British colonial legislation.

The commissioners never descended from this peak of influence during the 1760's. Although the Grenville administration lost power in 1765 and its successor repealed the Stamp Act, two of the most influential commissioners, Edward Hooper and William Musgrave, remained in office. The continuity in the customs board guaranteed that regardless of the ideas of a particular ministry, one important group of commissioners would continue to think in the same way they always had about America and American revenue. Assuredly, when the Chatham ministry, and Charles Townshend in particular, again offered them the chance to affect colonial customs, the customs commissioners again proposed significant departures from the old system. At least two of the measures connected with the Townshend Duties, the establishment of an American customs board and the legalization of writs of assistance, owed almost as much to the revenue board as had the Sugar Act.

THE TOWNSHEND DUTIES

Oliver M. Dickerson deemed the creation of an American customs board, with its jurisdiction separate and independent from that of the English customs commission, England's most fateful decision. A fateful decision, Dickerson noted, in its intent and in its conse-

---

vincial vice-admiralty courts and could not hear appeals from them. Indeed, before the Sugar Act allowed prosecutions for seizures in the North American court, both the attorney and solicitor generals had averred that offenses under the Navigation Acts could be tried only in the territory where the offense was committed. The Sugar Act allowed prosecutions in the "supercourt," the provincial common-law courts, or the provincial vice-admiralty courts.

quences. An American customs commission to gain an American revenue manifested England's deliberate intention to penalize the Americans. The new board presided only over American revenue, while the West Indian islands remained under the authority of the English commissioners. Hitherto all imperial legislation had included both America and the West Indies—the Stamp Act for example. But the new board signaled America's separation from the general imperial system and implied that America, especially wicked, needed to be watched and coerced more than the rest of the empire. In its consequences, according to Dickerson, the establishment of the commission proved yet more damaging to British prestige than earlier British action. The new customs officers who settled in the colonies to work for, and in, the new board proved some of the sharpest racketeers in history. They used every means at their disposal to further their own ends and seized, on any pretext, ships whose captains had no intention of defying the laws of trade. Ruthless, irresponsible, greedy, and grasping, they provoked the enmity of Henry Laurens and framed John Hancock on a trumped-up charge. Indeed, dishonest operations of the customs racketeers proved a cause of the American Revolution.[55]

On April 16, 1767, Charles Lowndes, secretary to the treasury, started the official train of these momentous events. He addressed a request to the commissioners of customs. "I am also to acquaint you," Lowndes stated, "that their Ldps. are desirous to receive from you any matters that you may have to suggest or propose relative

[55] Oliver M. Dickerson, "England's Most Fateful Decision," *The New England Quarterly*, XXII (1949), 388-394, and *The Navigation Acts and the American Revolution* (Philadelphia, 1951).

to the establishment of a board of customs in America."[56] Lowndes' letter suggests that the treasury initiated the plan for an American customs board, as had the secretary of state that for the Proclamation of 1763. Charles Townshend, chancellor of the exchequer and the most important minister at the treasury in April of 1767, probably formulated the basic idea. As early as 1754, when a junior member of the board of trade, Townshend had proposed to remodel colonial government by providing incomes to the colonial governors, judges, and other royal officers independent from the control of colonial legislatures, "to which," according to Sir Lewis Namier and John Brooke, "the raising of a revenue by Act of the British Parliament became a necessary corollary." By February 1, 1767, Townshend's ideas had evidently expanded to include the creation of a separate board of customs in America to superintend there the collection of the duties he hoped to raise.[57] But if the entire scheme came from the fertile brain of Charles Townshend and if he faced little political difficulty in pushing it through the "tessellated" Chatham ministry, the administrative problems remained. Would the British customs board approve such a plan? The treasury had so often accepted customs recommendations, even to the smallest detail, and had so often hesitated to act against customs wishes, that Townshend would have faced extraordinary difficulties—far more than any presented by the "pro-American" cabinet members—without the commissioners' sanction.

Edward Hooper and Sir William Musgrave, two of

[56] Charles Lowndes to the customs commissioners, Apr. 16, 1767: P.R.O., T. 11/28, p. 139.
[57] Sir Lewis Namier and John Brooke, *Charles Townshend* (New York, 1964), pp. 37, 172-186, and App. A.

the more prominent commissioners, would never have endorsed any revenue scheme they distrusted. Hooper, a customs commissioner since 1748, could boast nineteen years of continuous service, years in which he had bearded the Duke of Newcastle and challenged the policy of the Marquis of Rockingham. Hooper loved the service too much to acquiesce blindly in distasteful policies. His colleague, Sir William Musgrave, would have defended equally staunchly customs' rights, for he was equally concerned for the service. Indeed, at any time, day or night, he was ready to attend to any problem concerning the service regardless of personal convenience. Always available for serious politicians who needed advice, Musgrave later counseled Shelburne as Hooper had advised Newcastle. Both of these men, the one with twenty-two years' administrative experience, the other with four, would have opposed the American plan had it not suited them.

So would the new customs secretary who had succeeded the deceased William Wood.[58] Edward Stanley had never hesitated to speak out where either his own or the service's interests were involved. He had not hesitated to berate a minor customs official for politicking on the wrong side. Once he even fired from his office a supernumerary clerk who had secured the position through the powerful patronage of the treasury lords. When on another occasion the Duke of Newcastle claimed that the custom house took excessive fees, Stanley defied Newcastle.[59] Furthermore, were Stanley not an assertive

[58] Stanley succeeded Wood indirectly, for John Freemantle assumed the secretaryship directly upon Wood's death. Freemantle's tenure, however, lasted only a year.

[59] Stanley averred that his fees "were only such, as have been received by all of my predecessors, they are collected under the

man, were he not jealous of his rights and concerned over the welfare of the service, he would yet have had precedent in opposing American policy. His predecessor, William Wood, had spoken boldly at one time against American ministerial policy and suffered no repercussions.[60]

The customs, however, not only approved but warmly endorsed the Townshend plan. After deliberating fourteen days the commissioners presented forceful reasons in its favor. Their report opened by stating that the great distance from America rendered correspondence with officers there "very tedious & liable to great uncertainty & interruption." "Negligent, partial or corrupt officers" used their freedom from close supervision to evade orders, and good officers were discouraged for want of support. "The truth of this general observation has been long known & felt," the commissioners added. The difficulties under which revenue collectors labored had reached unprecedented heights. Attacked by mobs and even criminally prosecuted in colonial courts, they needed a board less remote than the one in England to look after their interests. The institution of surveyors general in America could not overcome the difficulties of distance. Although the customs commissioners considered the surveyors general necessary under present

---

authority of the patents of the collectors & comptrollers, and I believe have been taken ever since the passing of the act of navigation, & the act of the 7 & 8 Wm. 3, and I have always given receipts for the money paid me." See Edward Stanley to Duke of Newcastle, Oct. 14, 1756: B.M., MSS Add. 32,868.

[60] Wood had declared openly in January 1764 that he opposed the ministry's American plans. "I conceive you want information of several things from the Plantations," he stated, and hoped that "every [th]ing which may have been thought of respecting the Plantations may be deferred to another year." See Ch. 2, n. 50.

conditions, the latter could not be authorized to give the necessary "decisive orders & countenance to their inferior officers," because such action would be misrepresented in England. Yet the successful conduct of the extensive customs business in America depended on those very officers. The English board could only judge matters in the light of surveyors general's reports, while those very surveyors general lacked power to discipline or reward subordinates. "The just application of rewards & punishments are the great means of securing the faithfull discharge of duty in the officers of the revenue," the commissioners noted. Punishment was as necessary as reward, yet when guilt was discovered and a charge clearly made, the distance rendered punishment subject to "difficulty and delay." An American board could surmount not only these troubles, but would save enough money to pay its own way. The king, authorized by an act of Parliament, could put the American customs under the care of proper persons by means of a commission under the Great Seal: "such commissioners to have the same power in America as are at present vested in this board with respect to the several acts of navigation trade and revenue." The new board might thus solve many problems. The English commissioners emphatically repeated their conclusions at the end of their report:

> The experience the board of customs in England has from time to time had of the many and great difficulties attending their management in parts so remote, leaves us no room to doubt of the great utility of establishing a board of customs in America, with ample powers under the ultimate control of the treasury.[61]

[61] Customs commissioners to treasury, Apr. 30, 1767: P.R.O., T. 1/459, ff. 83-86.

The treasury lords read and highly approved this report the day after it came into their hands, but also asked for more particular information.[62] In June they requested an outline of the intended organization of a North American customs board and an estimate of its expense. They further wished to know the number of officers now in America who might be dismissed and whose salaries would help pay for the new establishment.[63] The customs commissioners responded quickly. They recommended five American commissioners, a secretary, chief clerk, register of seizures, a second clerk, two additional clerks, a solicitor with a chief clerk and copying clerks, a cashier and paymaster with clerical staff, comptrollers and a clerical staff, two inspectors general attendant on the board, and an inspector of imports and exports and register of shipping. They estimated costs at £4,500. The commissioners believed the new institution, despite its initially heavy cost, would eliminate enough officers on the English establishment to save £2,491. They thought, however, to include the West Indies under the jurisdiction of the new American board.[64]

The treasury lords considered this second report on July 22, called in the customs commissioners to discuss it, and approved every part except the inclusion of the West Indies under the new commission. A decision about this area the treasury postponed until July 29, when the lords summoned representatives of London mer-

[62] P.R.O., T. 29/38, f. 182, minute of May 1, 1767. See also Grey Cooper to the customs commissioners, May 1, 1767: P.R.O., T. 11/28, p. 140.

[63] P.R.O., T. 29/38, f. 205, minute of June 23, 1767.

[64] Sydney Papers, vol. 7, Clements Library, contain the formal response of the commissioners and their estimate. P.R.O., T. 1/459, ff. 206-207 is a more abbreviated response.

chants trading to the sugar colonies. They in turn
objected so strongly to putting the West Indies under
American jurisdiction that the treasury determined to
continue the old system in the islands.[65] Only the continental colonies would have their own customs commissioners.

These various interchanges formed the origins of the
ill-omened American customs commission under the
Great Seal of England. Such a commission, duly authorized by Parliament, ventured to America with the results
described by Dickerson. Treasury pressure on the customs
probably affected the arrangements little, if at all. Indeed,
the entire board had resisted some pressure. It absolutely refused the treasury request to prepare instructions for the new commissioners. The "commission, and
the laws," Edward Stanley told Grey Cooper, "will describe their duty, and the powers, and authorities with
which they are invested."[66] In general, however, the commissioners had supported the plan for an American
board, and their endorsement had rendered nearly certain its establishment.

Their endorsement had been necessary, but perhaps
not their creative imagination. No clear evidence shows
they initially suggested the measure, as they had the
Sugar Act. On the contrary, the burden of evidence favors Charles Townshend. But the commissioners, at the
least, turned Townshend's dreams into reality, much as
Whately and his colleagues had done with the Stamp

---

[65] P.R.O., T. 29/38, ff. 220-221, minute of July 29, 1767.

[66] Edward Stanley to Grey Cooper, Aug. 26, 1767: P.R.O., T. 1/459,
ff. 140-141. Of course the revenue board did provide the new secretary to the American board such information in its files as might
prove useful, and its inspector general of imports and exports
prepared the forms necessary for keeping American accounts.

Act. The revenue board contributed even more to a second piece of legislation connected with the Townshend Duties, the writs of assistance. The chancellor of the exchequer's fertile brain may have conceived of certain import duties for the colonies and an American board to collect them, but the customs commissioners proposed the method Townshend hopefully adopted to make the collection easier. They suggested that writs of assistance be legalized as a powerful prop to the customs officers in America and urged their plan strongly to the ministry. At their continued insistence, the ministry acquiesced.

Before 1767 these writs, so condemned by James Otis, could not be used legally in the colonies, and when illegally used proved ineffective in the apprehension of either smugglers or smuggled goods. The customs officers' often futile attempts to find merchandise already landed compared to locking the stable door after the horse had been stolen. Grenville's efforts to tighten the colonial customs system in 1763 and 1764 brought home to the English customs commissioners the need for more effective powers to revenue officers. Their chance to secure these powers came during the Chatham administration and Townshend chancellorship.

In 1766 the collector and comptroller of New London moaned their lack of sufficient authority. The customs commissioners, heeding the complaint, asked the attorney general to define the specific powers of American customs officers. Did the act of 7 and 8 William and Mary permit these officers "to enter houses & warehouses to search for and seize any prohibited or run goods without a writ of assistants"? If not, from what colonial court could a writ of assistance be procured? Attorney General De Grey indicated that the statute allowed colonial cus-

toms officers the same authority as their English colleagues to enter shops, houses, and other buildings to
search out goods. He noted, however, that the provincial
officers did not actually enjoy these rights. The English
officers received their writs of assistance from the court of
exchequer in England. This court did not send its process
to the plantations, "nor is there any process in the plantations that corresponds, with the description in the act
of K. W."[67] American officers in fact lacked sufficient
power to search and could not obtain it without an act
of Parliament.

The customs commissioners urged such an act. They
submitted to the treasury "whether it may not be expedient to have the interposition of Parliament for granting the proper means to the officers of the revenue in
America, on the several points mentioned in the case
inclosed."[68] The treasury at first did nothing, and
the commissioners pressed their case further. On November 22 they again wrote the treasury and enclosed
another example of Boston obstruction to the collector
and comptroller of the port. Again they cited De Grey's
report, and again urged an act of Parliament.[69] The
second request evidently succeeded, for the act that pre-
scribed the Townshend Duties in 1767 took cognizance
of the customs' propositions. It empowered any "superior
or supreme court of justice having jurisdiction within
such colony or plantation respectively," to grant, upon
application, writs of assistance to customs officers.[70]

These American writs, unlike those issued by the

[67] Attorney General William De Grey's report is in P.R.O., T.
1/453, ff. 187-194.

[68] Customs commissioners to treasury, Oct. 31, 1766: P.R.O., T.
1/453, f. 185.

[69] Customs commissioners to treasury, Nov. 22, 1766: *Ibid.*, ff.
169-174.

[70] The statute is 7 Geo. III, c. 46.

exchequer in England, resembled a general warrant. England had declared such documents illegal in 1765, and an English writ of assistance could not, in any event, be applied to the interior of the country. Not so in America. The writ of assistance drawn up by the collector and comptroller of New York showed the broad powers American customs officers might acquire. The writ permitted both of them, in concert with a constable or other public officer, to enter any "ship, boat, or other vessell, as also any house, warehouse, shop, cellar, or other place in this colony and in cases of resistance to break open doors, chests, trunks, and other packages, and from thence to bring away any kind of merchandize whatsoever prohibited to be imported or exported, or whereof the customs or other duties have not been and shall not be duly paid."[71] Thus a customs officer of New York City could journey to Albany, or German Flats, or anywhere else in the colony and break and enter any building he suspected of harboring illegal goods. He could further require colonial officers to aid this arbitrary process. No one in England, least of all a customs officer, enjoyed such power in 1767.

As with some other colonial measures, the power Britain hoped for in theory it failed to attain in fact. The customs commissioners, Hooper and Musgrave foremost among them, through persistent application had brought writs of assistance to the aid of their American co-workers.[72] American courts, however, never allowed the royal revenue officials to reach out and grasp this

[71] For this writ see P.R.O., T. 1/429, ff. 54-55.

[72] These two men and Commissioner Pennington signed the first report, and the same two and Commissioner Frederick signed the second one. Since neither Pennington nor Frederick appears to have been so active as Hooper and Musgrave, the latter probably composed both reports.

aid. Customs officers unsuccessfully tried to secure writs from the supreme courts of Maryland, Georgia, Pennsylvania, New York (after an initial success), Virginia, Connecticut, Rhode Island, and South Carolina.[73] That the plan failed, however, in no way lessened colonial animosity. Indeed, like the stamps that were never sold or the *Gaspee* investigation that failed to find the guilty, writs of assistance encouraged American opposition to Britain. Many continental colonists, aware that customs officials held an objectionable authority given them by the mother country, resented the officials, the authority, and the nation that spawned both. As a supreme court justice in Maryland said to the collector and comptroller of Pocomoke, Maryland, when they asked for the writs: "let them apply for general warrants . . . when they want them."[74]

The customs board must have produced tension equal to that excited by its American "general warrants" when it came to examine the regulations governing colonial coastal shipping. In March of 1765 Treasury Secretary Whately transmitted to the revenue commissioners a complaint from merchants engaged in this trade. Colonial commerce suffered from numerous obstructions, the complaint stipulated, some of which could be removed without loss to the revenue. Could not goods be carried from one colony to another without cockets or suffrances, and could not vessels from Great Britain be exempted from search until in port? The customs commissioners replied mainly in the negative. They conceded that small coasting vessels without decks, loaded with Ameri-

[73] See the numerous failures recorded in P.R.O., T. 1/501, ff. 173-180, 265-302.

[74] Collector and comptroller of Pocomoke, Md., to the American customs board, June 12, 1769: P.R.O., T. 1/492, f. 62.

can products not subject to duty on importation or exportation, and not prohibited to be exported from America could sail from one colony to another without cockets or suffrances. They refused to consider loosening the system further. Laws requiring vessels to be searched only after reaching harbor, they argued, inevitably dampened the vigilance of the naval officers. These officers should, however, be instructed to conduct themselves with discretion and not interrrupt ships proceeding straight to port.[75] The treasury accepted the commissioners' views. Parliament passed a law authorizing coasting vessels to trade between colonies without cockets or suffrances—the limit of the commissioners' concessions.[76]

The customs board now adamantly refused to budge in the face of continued colonial complaints. Charles Garth, agent for South Carolina, presented a memorial to the treasury in January of 1766. It asserted that coasting vessels carrying indigo, rice, and the staples of South Carolina to Charleston, the general port of export, had been seized in port because they lacked the clearance papers necessary for seagoing vessels. Seizures of these ships followed by condemnation in the vice-admiralty court, Garth explained, had cost the planters much vexation, time, and money. These vessels, although engaged only in the coasting trade, required decks for security. Without such decks, coasters faced the possibility that bad weather might ruin their cargoes. Furthermore, the many dangerous reefs and shoals of the Carolina coast-

[75] Customs commissioners to the treasury, Mar. 22, 1765: P.R.O., T. 1/441, f. 325. The treasury failed to read the report until a month later. See P.R.O., T. 29/36, pp. 315-316, minute of Apr. 22, 1765.

[76] The statute is 5 Geo. III, c. 45, section 26.

al waters often forced coasters out to sea. An open-decked boat dared not sail far from the coast, although it often needed to do so. The agent therefore asked the treasury to allow owners of coasting ships to deck such ships and to give bond only once a year against engaging in fraudulent practices.[77] The treasury referred the memorial to the customs commissioners. They in turn completely rejected Garth's representations. The commissioners stipulated that parliamentary statute already had taken care of all difficulties. Further relief, unnecessary in any event, could not be granted "without opening a door to continual frauds, & abuses, & leaving the revenue destitute of that security provided for it, by the act of navigation, and to which the coasting trade of Great Britain continues subject."[78] The treasury followed the lead of its subordinate. On December 2 the lords commissioners read "and approved" the customs report.[79] Garth may have been right or wrong in this particular case—the coasting trade may or may not have been suffering under the restrictions he mentioned—but right or wrong, suffering or not, an adverse report by the commissioners of the English customs had settled the matter.[80]

[77] Memorial of Charles Garth, Jan. 16, 1766: P.R.O., T. 1/453, ff. 176-177.

[78] Customs commissioners to treasury, Nov. 27, 1766: *Ibid.*, ff. 174-175.

[79] P.R.O., T. 29/38, f. 108, minute of Dec. 2, 1766.

[80] Considering the information available to the English customs board, it seems justified in suspecting the merchants' petitions. American customs officers constantly reported on the various vexatious obstructions to the prevention of smuggling. In 1767 Edward Stanley informed Treasury Secretary Thomas Bradshaw of a ridiculous situation in South Carolina, and Bradshaw passed the information on to Admiralty Secretary Philip Stephens. A naval captain stationed in Charleston encountered grave difficulties in securing condemnation of the vessels he had seized for engaging in illicit trade.

The English customs commissioners, often overlooked
in studies of events which led to the American Revolution, were among the most important subministers involved in colonial policy during the 1760's. They proposed
the Sugar Act, the establishment of the vice-admiralty
court at Halifax, and legalization of writs of assistance.
They constructed the American customs board on the
basis of ministerial recommendations and until 1767
directed the American customs system with an eye to
tightening regulations. Indeed, they fulfilled at one time
or another all three of the subministerial roles in imperial affairs. Through specific recommendations they
transformed the ministerial idea of closing loopholes in
the American customs network into specific measures,
such as the act of Parliament relating to coasters. They
breathed life, through their command of administrative
procedure, into the Townshend plan for an American
customs board. They initiated important measures—
the Sugar Act and writs of assistance—which ministries
adopted.[81]

The attorney general of the colony could not prosecute smuggling
cases before the court of vice-admiralty, because he also held the position of judge of vice-admiralty. His dual capacity negated efforts to
stop illicit trade. Bradshaw expressed the treasury's desire that the
admiralty appoint someone other than the attorney general as judge
of the vice-admiralty court, "that the interest of the crown may not
suffer." Nearly a year passed before the admiralty acted. In May
of 1768 Stephens finally informed the governor of South Carolina
that the admiralty wished the attorney general not to act as judge
of vice-admiralty or, if judge of vice-admiralty, not to act as attorney general. This affair constituted only one of the many obstacles the English customs board faced daily. See Thomas Bradshaw to Philip Stephens, Aug. 25, 1767: P.R.O., Adm. 1/4286, and
Philip Stephens to Lord Charles Greville Montague, May 4, 1768:
P.R.O., Adm. 2/1057, f. 276.

[81] W. R. Ward, "Civil Servants," *E.H.R.*, LXX (1955), 25-54, asserts

Years of Multiple Participation

Although their influence on American policy lessened between 1768 and 1775, when the American department took over the direction of colonial affairs, the customs commissioners and their subministerial colleagues had momentously affected the events of the 1760's. Multiple subministerial participation had turned the general policies behind the Proclamation of 1763 and the Stamp Act into specific documents and had suggested and created the Sugar Act and much of the policy associated with the Townshend Duties. Two undersecretaries to the American department tended to assume, under the secretary, the direction of colonial affairs after 1770, but they only continued along the trail already blazed by their colleagues. The vigorous subministers of the 1760's, a real administrative force, pushed Britain as quickly toward Lexington Green as the pamphlets, the bluster, the parliamentary oratory, and the succession of ministries that marched in and out of Whitehall.

---

that they exerted little influence on policy before the 1780's. While they may have lacked political influence, their enormous importance to the administrative developments of the 1760's belies Ward's belief.

CHAPTER FOUR

Concentration of Influence: The American Department in the Early Seventies

DURING the 1760's the English customs commissioners held the spotlight in proposals for raising a revenue through new customs procedure. They relinquished this position to others, however, in the Proclamation of 1763 and the Stamp Act. But in all cases—customs, Proclamation. Stamp Act—groups of subministers worked together to plan and execute a policy. In the 1770's these cooperative endeavors diminished. From 1768 to 1775, but especially after 1772, the American department commanded more and more of the ministry's colonial program. Under the firm leadership of the Earl of Hillsborough it began to control colonial policy. Hillsborough's successor, Lord Dartmouth, gathered all the threads of American patronage, sewed them together, and enhanced control.[1] The power these two peers acquired their subordinates exercised. Indeed, from 1772 to 1775 the undersecretaries of state to the American department, John Pownall and William Knox, loomed ever larger in British-American relations.

Knox added yet a new dimension to the subministerial role in this tragedy, that of ministerial propagandist. Both he and his colleague Pownall exercised the first of the subministerial functions under Lord Hillsborough: they implemented and administered previously established policy. Under Lord Dartmouth, whose tenure began in 1772, they shaped general policy into specific

[1] For this chapter in the development of the American department, see Sosin, *Whitehall*, pp. 181-210.

acts and proposed measures that the ministry accepted, the second and third of the characteristic labors of minor men. But Knox also defended vigorously through pamphlets perhaps the two most important measures of the period, the Quebec Act and the Boston Port Bill. Although Thomas Whately's pen had earlier lauded Grenville's ministry, Whately had reacted to criticism more as a private person than as an official entrusted with a duty. The North ministry, on the other hand, employed Undersecretary Knox specifically to show its actions in the best light. Political propaganda thus came to complement the subministerial work of proposing and implementing departmental and ministerial decisions.

The most important of these decisions occupied the years of the Dartmouth administration, a period of unceasing subministerial activity. The frequent absences of the noble lord left nearly the entire administrative responsibility for the American department with the undersecretaries, and Knox and Pownall must have opened each fresh dispatch with increasing apprehension. They had both worked hard enough for Hillsborough, had liked him, and had seen him topple as a result of the sordid machinations of a group of unscrupulous speculators in western American lands. Now western lands, eastern lands, and the Atlantic coastal waters of America displayed a remarkable and continuous propensity to trouble the colonial department.

Indeed, the waters off New England proved more troublesome at first to Hillsborough's successor than the interior settlements. Americans defied Britain on its traditional element and wrecked the customs ship *Gaspee* in the first year of his tenure. It would be the American department's duty under its new head to help form a committee to investigate the incident. This committee, in turn, would sting the Americans. Although in the end it accomplished nothing—it never discovered guilty persons and died in America almost at birth—the *Gaspee* commission would serve notice of the British government's hardening determination to curb violence and punish persons who destroyed Crown property. The Stamp Act rioters as well as others equally defiant had escaped retribution. The commission intended to catch the latest despoilers and ship them to England charged with treason. It would thus foreshadow ominously the more effective punishment Britain meted out later to the port of Boston. It would also, even more than the Proclamation of 1763, be the creature of John Pownall.

In June of 1772 Americans, enraged at the customs officers who harassed their shipping and persecuted their leading citizens, stormed the revenue schooner *Gaspee* and left it a burning, useless hulk. When news of the conflagration reached England the attorney general and solicitor general examined the legal questions the violent affair posed. They finally described the burning as treason—making war on the king—and resolved that those men suspected of it be sent to England for trial. On August 20 the cabinet decided to prepare a commission appointing persons to inquire into the burning and discover the guilty parties. It also submitted that the king offer pardon and reward to anyone pointing out the traitors.[2] Next day the privy council ordered the attorney general and solicitor general to draft the commission and the king's proclamation.[3] At this point Dartmouth, the American secretary, should have stepped into the center of work so vital to his department. But Dartmouth departed London for his country home in Staffordshire

2 Cabinet meeting of Aug. 20, 1772: Dartmouth Papers II/386.
3 P.R.O., Privy Council 2/116, pp. 421-424.

and left the Whitehall offices to Undersecretary John Pownall.

The attorney general and solicitor general knew little about preparing a commission of inquiry for an American colony, so Pownall sent them "such papers as he apprehends may be useful for their information upon this occasion." The undersecretary's several documents included examples of commissioners appointed to inquire into conditions in colonies "that have fallen into great disorder and confusion."[4] Fortified with this information, the lawyers drafted the commission and presented it to the council,[5] which on August 26 approved it and the proclamation. It also ordered Dartmouth to prepare the latter and a warrant for passing the commission under the Great Seal. The absence of the secretary of state, of course, necessitated that John Pownall execute council orders. He finished swiftly and informed his vacationing chief of the work. "The warrant your lordship will observe," Pownall explained, "has been already signed by the King, but it can go no farther until it has been countersigned by your lordship and the words at the end of it—*by His Majesty's commands* will inform your lordship where to put your name."[6] That Dartmouth had to be told where to append his signature to work prepared by someone else speaks volumes about the importance of the secretary of state vis-à-vis Undersecretary Pownall to the *Gaspee* inquiry.

Yet Pownall could not rest. Other commission matters still beckoned. The attorney general believed the commis-

[4] Pownall's report and list of precedents is in the Wedderburn Papers 1/7, Clements Library.

[5] P.R.O., P.C. 2/116, pp. 424-426. The commission may be found on pp. 426-427, and the proclamation on pp. 428-430.

[6] John Pownall to Earl of Dartmouth, Aug. 26, 1772: Dartmouth Papers II/394.

sioners should be instructed under the signet and sign manual. Pownall drew up the instructions.[7] The cabinet determined to require General Gage to assist the commissioners upon request and to inform the governor of Rhode Island (one of the commissioners) of Gage's orders. Pownall, not Dartmouth, wrote the letter to the Rhode Island governor.[8] The undersecretary finally insured that the circumstances surrounding the commission receive proper publicity. "I presume your lordship will think it advisable that there should be some notification of the comm[issione]rs & proclamat[io]n in the Gazette," Pownall wrote Dartmouth, "and I have accordingly suggested to Mr. Eden for Lord Suffolk's directions upon what appears to me necessary on this occasion."[9] Thus Pownall dispatched nearly all the business relative to Britain's newer, tougher policy.

Both Pownall and Knox found as much work in 1773 as the *Gaspee* affair of the previous year had required, but work of less immediate consequence. Usually they either continued with colonial plans already underway or routinely administered matters that did not particularly estrange British-American relations. All during 1773, nonetheless, undersecretarial authority waxed. Pownall, practically on his own authority, altered the powers of the commissary of Indian affairs, John Campbell, and directed the governor of New York in the proper use of

[7] John Pownall to Earl of Dartmouth, Aug. 27, 1772: Dartmouth Papers II/397. The instructions may be seen in P.R.O., C.O. 5/1284, ff. 195-198. They contain six articles, the third of which stresses the civil magistrate's power to arrest anyone found guilty in order that the guilty person or persons be shipped to England for trial.

[8] See the letter to Governor John Wanton, Sept. 4, 1772: P.R.O., C.O. 5/1284, ff. 187-194.

[9] John Pownall to Earl of Dartmouth, Sept. 1, 1772: Dartmouth Papers II/412.

troops.[10] In yet another instance he came forth with a plan designed to tighten British control over Massachusetts, the recall of Governor Hutchinson. His method of broaching this scheme and the ministry's quick and cordial reception suggest that the undersecretarial impact on colonial policy was beginning to exceed even that of the undersecretaries in the 1760's.

Concerned over the turbulence and disorder in Massachusetts John Pownall wished to recall Governor Hutchinson as a prelude to firm action. Determined upon his course, Pownall approached Lord Dartmouth:

> I am more & more convinced that it would be both a credit & advantage to Govr. Hutchinson if he was ordered home to lay before the King a state of his govt., & that it would be of great utility in any further steps that may be taken regarding that province. Lord North I think is doubtfull of the utility of it, but will acquiesce if you approve it. If you do I think it should be proposed and determined in the cabinet, & therefore I beg your lordship's directions whether I should put it upon the list of cabinet business next Wednesday.[11]

Dartmouth followed the lead, but Pownall did not even need, in the end, to bring his idea before the cabinet. He visited North privately, urged his proposal, and on August 12, 1773, carried the point with a "doubtful" first lord of the treasury. Matters were so arranged that Hutchinson should appear to be coming to England at his own request. The ministry (and Pownall) had fully approved his conduct and had no intention of implying

[10] See pp. 74-76.

[11] John Pownall to Earl of Dartmouth, Aug. 5, 1773: Dartmouth Papers I, part II/871.

dissatisfaction, but it dispatched recall instructions.[12]

"Recall" preluded yet firmer action, for the next year witnessed passage of two of the major causes of the American Revolution, the Boston Port Bill and the Quebec Act. The two undersecretaries, Knox and Pownall, overwhelmingly influenced these measures. Pownall proposed the Port Bill and almost on his own took the necessary steps to render it effective. Undersecretary Knox played the key role in drafting the Quebec Act, and at the behest of the ministry advertised both it and the Port Bill to the British public.

In 1770, the year he entered the American department as an undersecretary, William Knox proposed a plan to maintain order in the tumultuous colony of Massachusetts Bay. Knox believed his scheme would prompt the people of the colony "to pay obedience," and would render disobedience "injurious to themselves." He intended to reward those individuals "well disposed to the sovereignty of Great Britain" and to punish "those who are arriving at independency." An act of Parliament should require all ships' masters who cleared their vessels from any harbor or port in the plantations, or fished anywhere north of the Penobscot, to take an oath acknowledging the sovereignty of the "imperial Crown & Parliament of Great Britain." The masters should also admit in this oath the right of king and Parliament to legislate for the colonies. Other men—like those wishing a license for Indian trade—might also be required to take the oath.[13] In retrospect Knox's plan appears impractical. In all probability it would have angered the Americans, increased their dissatisfaction with British rule, and

---

[12] John Pownall to Earl of Dartmouth, Aug. 12, 1773: Dartmouth Papers I, part II/872.

[13] Knox's plan, dated only 1770, is in Dartmouth Papers II/331.

would have defeated its avowed purpose of intensifying loyalty.

But if the "loyalty" scheme for the Bay Colony never found its way into British policy, Knox's colleague later forwarded suggestions for Massachusetts which the ministry fully accepted. Four years after the Knox plan, the Bay Colony shouted its "disloyalty" far louder than it had in 1770. Patriots dumped tea into Boston harbor and the British ministers intended retribution. One of the methods they chose, the Boston Port Bill, came to them from Undersecretary of State John Pownall. William Knox attributed the proposal to Pownall, and although Knox sometimes confused his "facts," credibility favors the undersecretary in this instance.[14] Indeed, a memorandum of Pownall's strengthens the Knox assertion nearly beyond doubt. Although undated, the memorandum referred to the "measures proposed in respect to the town & people of Boston." Written sometime before February 17, 1774, and probably after January 29 of the same year,[15] it suggested four immediate steps to "prevent or defeat resistance" to the closing of the port: (1) send without delay to America troops under orders to relieve American garrisons there; (2) reinforce the North American naval squadron with two ships; (3) transport General Gage with the troops to Boston at once; and (4) require the navy to cooperate fully with customs officials in order that no ship could be unloaded without proper authority.[16]

[14] "Proceedings in Relation to the American Colonies," H.M.C., *Rept. on MSS Var. Coll.*, VI, 257.

[15] Dartmouth Papers II/799 shows that on Jan. 29 the cabinet determined to punish Boston. Pownall's scheme, therefore, must have been drafted after this meeting.

[16] Dartmouth Papers II/1044.

The ministry implemented each one of these suggested steps. One regiment of troops scheduled to leave Britain on June 15 was ordered instead to depart on April 15 so as to sail with three other regiments.[17] The four regiments, previously assigned to various parts of America, were now posted to Boston.[18] Instructions went to the admiralty on February 17 to reinforce the North American squadron with two guardships.[19] On April 1 Pownall urged the attorney general to pass the warrant for General Gage's commission as governor of Massachusetts. Four days later the admiralty began to prepare a suitable ship to carry the new governor to Massachusetts "with all possible dispatch."[20] Finally, instructions went to the admiral commanding in North America to "give the officers of the revenue all proper assistance."[21] Thus John Pownall proposed the Boston Port Bill, and all the measures the ministry adopted to enforce it.

He further shared in the formation of another piece of legislation that entered the statutes in the same year, the Quebec Act. This imperial measure differed markedly from the Boston Port Bill. Although the colonists interpreted the Quebec Act, like the Port Bill, as a coercive measure, plans for a change in Quebec's status had been discussed in ministerial circles long before American patriots dumped tea into Boston Harbor. The Rockingham

[17] Viscount Barrington to Earl of Dartmouth, Feb. 14, 1774: P.R.O., C.O. 5/247, f. 91.

[18] Earl of Dartmouth to admiralty, Apr. 2, 1774: P.R.O., C.O. 5/250, ff. 77-78.

[19] Earl of Dartmouth to admiralty, Feb. 17, 1774: P.R.O., Adm. 1/4129, letter 131.

[20] John Pownall to the attorney general, Apr. 1, 1774: P.R.O., C.O. 5/250, f. 77, and Earl of Dartmouth to admiralty, Apr. 2, 1774: P.R.O., C.O. 5/250, f. 78.

[21] Philip Stephens to Adm. John Montagu, Apr. 11, 1774: P.R.O., Adm. 2/548, p. 402.

government of 1765 first examined seriously the situation in Quebec. It realized that the Proclamation of 1763 left in doubt the type of law to be administered in the province and failed to provide for the free exercise of the Roman Catholic religion. Governor Murray of Canada, unable to abolish the customary French law, had compromised by permitting the pleading of French or English law, or both, in civil suits, but had allowed only English law in criminal cases.[22] In 1765 the board of trade requested a change in the Canadian judicial structure. At the same time the attorney general and solicitor general declared Catholics in Canada exempt from English penal laws against their faith.[23] Government action began. The Rockingham ministry accepted some of the plantation office recommendations: it allowed jury service and the bar to both English and French on equal terms. Attorney General Yorke then reported on the laws of Canada to the privy council on April 14, 1776. He submitted that criminal law should remain English, but that French law should determine all suits relating to property, regardless of the date of transaction.[24] He also urged appointment of French Canadian magistrates.[25] The privy council approved Yorke's report and instructed John Pownall to draft additional instructions for the governor of Quebec according to its recommendations. With Yorke's aid Pownall outlined a comprehensive plan for Canada. Yet the plan never passed the privy council

[22] The governor's ordinance of Sept. 17, 1764, is in Shortt and Doughty, *Canada Documents*, I, 149-152.

[23] *Canada Documents*, I, 171-172, contains the legal report.

[24] Gov. James Murray's ordinance allowed French law in civil suits only if the cause of action arose before 1764.

[25] The attorney general and solicitor general's report (written by Charles Yorke) is in Shortt and Doughty, *Canada Documents*, I, 174-178.

because Lord Chancellor Northington blocked it. Pownall's scheme, contained, nevertheless, some clauses identical to those later found in the Quebec Act.[26] Because of Northington's obstinacy, the Rockingham attempt to straighten affairs in the former French colony without parliamentary action failed, but Pownall had outlined a fruitful course for future ministries.

They took at best, however, haphazard action until 1773.[27] In that year, "after a decade of discussion," the North ministry at last moved forward. The Quebec Act—primarily the responsibility of Solicitor General Wedderburn for its final wording—was introduced into the House of Lords by Lord Dartmouth in May of 1774. Undersecretary William Knox had spent much of the previous year preparing the measure. He seems to have done the lion's share of work on the bill, although he was of course familiar with Pownall's work.[28] Subministers had again hastened the American Revolution, although this time inadvertently. They had intended only to settle the just grievances of the French Canadians and to alleviate some of the problems of western American lands, rather than to threaten the American colonists.

Threatening, however, was the government's determination to abide by both the Quebec Act and the Port

[26] Pownall's plan is quoted in R. A. Humphreys and S. Morley Scott, "Lord Northington and the Laws of Canada," *Canadian Historical Review*, XIV (1933), 54-61. Most of the information on this Rockingham attempt to provide an early comprehensive settlement for Canada is taken from the Humphreys and Scott article, which covers pages 42-61.

[27] The Earl of Shelburne sent Maurice Morgann out to Canada to investigate Canadian laws when Shelburne held office as southern secretary under Chatham, but Morgann scarcely recommended any new or startling suggestions. See Shelburne Papers 64/525-551.

[28] Sosin, *Whitehall*, pp. 239-255, shows in detail the origins of the Quebec Act.

Bill, and to advertise widely its stand. The North ministry now employed the forceful pen of William Knox to publicize the two measures he and his colleague Pownall had done so much to create. No one could have presented the government's case to the public in pamphlet form better than Knox, who knew the measures as well as anyone else and who excelled in the art of polemics. Indeed, the ministry may have hired him in 1770 because the then American secretary of state, Lord Hillsborough, might have anticipated a use for his particular talents. Knox had more or less steadily pamphleteered for the previous ten years in favor of earlier colonial enactments as controversial as the ones he was now called upon to defend. In 1765 his pamphlet *Claim of the Colonies* had so vigorously espoused the Stamp Act, or at least Britain's right to legislate such a measure, that he lost his position. He had then moved into the Grenville faction as the American "expert" and produced a series of tracts during the next five years that argued strongly for parliamentary supremacy over America. The Rockinghams considered his work so potent that their polemical expert, Edmund Burke, had attempted to refute him, condemn the Grenville policy, and elevate the Rockingham ministry, all in reaction to one of Knox's pamphlets, *The Present State of the Nation*. In 1769 the future undersecretary had penned perhaps the ablest statement ever written favoring parliamentary supremacy over the colonies. Experience, ability, and familiarity with the material to be used, made Knox the obvious choice to vindicate two of the most important pieces of British legislation of the period 1763 to 1776.

Knox did both jobs well. In justification of the Quebec Act he pointed out the past British mistakes in Canada and described the hardships of the Canadians. He then drew a concise, clear picture of the benefits the new measure promised. Of course the Quebec Act, a wise statute designed rather to help French Canadians than to coerce American colonists, lent itself more easily to praise than the second measure, the Boston Port Bill.[29] The London merchants, who on earlier occasions had pressed the ministry to repeal American legislation possibly detrimental to trade, needed to be convinced of the necessity for the particular direction British policy had now taken. North understood the mercantile community might see in the Port Bill and the other Coercive Acts a threat to commerce because the colonists had responded to the legislation with nonimportation, nonexportation, and nonconsumption agreements.[30] Knox, therefore, had to persuade not only the public at large but an extremely powerful and vociferous group. His own convictions and his past experience enabled his *Interest of the Merchants and Manufacturers* to hammer the arguments home. The tract contended that British legislation neither intended to harm nor did harm the colonies. Knox maintained effectively that colonial wealth stemmed from credit extended to America by British merchants, but that the safe extension of credit depended upon the successful operation of British laws in the colonies. Without these laws merchants could never be assured a return for their money. Colonial defiance of Parliament's authority harmed everyone, and the men of commerce should

[29] See William Knox, *The Justice and Policy of the Late Act of Parliament, for making more Effectual Provision for the Government of the Province of Quebec, Asserted and Proved: and the Conduct of the Administration Respecting that Province Stated and Vindicated* (London, 1774).

[30] William Knox to Earl of Dartmouth, Nov. 15, 1774: H.M.C., *The Manuscripts of the Earl of Dartmouth* (3 vols., London, 1887-1896), II, 233.

search their real interests and refrain from despair at the first sign of decreased profits.[31]

The profits of some men, in fact, fell swiftly, for the Quebec Act and the Coercive Acts—of which the Boston Port Bill was a part—were the last pieces of major British colonial legislation before the outbreak of the American Revolution. These two measures, like the ones of the 1760's that had required multiple talents, had felt the subministerial touch constantly. One cannot help wondering what motivated the subministers, or more properly whether they acted after having assessed fully the nature of colonial problems and the probable implications of their work. What was their considered opinion, indeed, of the correct mother country–colony relationship, and did they conscientiously attempt to implement that opinion? Lack of evidence, unfortunately, forbids any definitive answer and often tantalizes more than it helps. Although prolific writers such as William Knox made clear their colonial attitudes, John Pownall's feelings toward the proper role of colonies within the British Empire yet remain obscure. Men like Thomas Whately, who knew colonial matters and colonial problems only through friends resident in North America (whose advice he chose occasionally to disregard), probably attuned their thoughts on the mother country–colony relationship to those of their political chiefs. Yet Maurice Morgann argued for far more restrictions on the colonies than his chief Lord Shelburne would have wished.

What of the customs commissioners? Edward Hooper made clear often enough his concern for the service and administrative efficiency, but was that his sole consid-

---

[31] See William Knox, *The Interest of the Merchants and Manufacturers of Great Britain in the Present Contest with the Colonies Stated and Considered* (London, 1774).

Concentration of Influence

eration in recommending, as he did, momentous changes in colonial customs procedure? Diligent search may someday unearth the documents necessary to answer fully such questions and put an end to speculation. The task ought to be worth the effort, for whatever the motivation, the subministers clearly led in the major pieces of imperial legislation of the 1760's and 1770's.

Hostilities with America now paid the fiddler's bill, and the minor men shifted from colonial policy to war.

CHAPTER FIVE

Cooperation during the War

THE subministers did not, and could not of course, dictate policy during actual hostilities. Their role was almost bound to diminish upon the outbreak of firing. Yet their activities during the war merit at least passing notice. They interpreted their superiors' commands to the military and civilian officials. They corresponded informally over a multitude of problems—supply, smuggling, impressment, postal dispatches—in order to straighten administrative entanglements. Britain's military effort suffered from poor direction by the home government, indifferent or incapable commanders in the field, gigantic problems of supply, and many more difficulties. Although men like Lord Sandwich exerted mighty efforts to rebuild and resupply the British navy for the unprecedented demands on it, he alone could not overcome the errors of Lord George Germain and his generals, the penny pinching of Lord North, and the failures at sea of supposedly able and experienced naval officers.[1] The subministers attempted to mitigate the force of these deficiencies. They did their best to win the war and their best—usually overlooked—often was better than that of their superiors.

[1] For a reappraisal of the Earl of Sandwich's work, see Mary B. Wickwire's unpublished dissertation, *Lord Sandwich and the King's Ships* (Yale, 1963). Germain, also, has been reappraised. Although Alan Valentine, *Lord George Germain* (Oxford, 1962), places much of the blame for the blunders of the American war upon the shoulders of the secretary. Gerald Saxon Brown, *The American Secretary, The Colonial Policy of Lord George Germain, 1775-1778* (Ann Arbor, 1963), credits Germain with intelligent handling of his department and the war effort, and blames the British generals mainly for the failures in America, at least to 1778.

Cooperation during the War

Indeed, had Lord Sandwich been able to find many admirals as eager to serve and as capable of serving at sea as Secretary Philip Stephens was at home the navy's role would have been far more effective. And the American Revolution could never have been suppressed without an effective navy. Even Lord North admitted to William Eden as war ominously approached that seapower would determine its outcome.[2] Holding the confidence of North, of Sandwich, and even of American Secretary Germain, Philip Stephens tried mightily to increase British seapower.[3]

Seapower, however, in part hinged upon manpower, and the navy never seemed to have enough sailors. Abominable living conditions for the enlisted personnel necessitated that the press gang largely supply the crews to man the navy's vessels. But obstacles to the press sometimes intolerably delayed the admiralty's issuing the necessary press warrants. Only Philip Stephens seemed able to act with the speed necessary in war when red tape impeded swiftness. In 1779 he plunged boldly forward. He ordered impressment on the coasts of Kent and Sussex without official authority and hoped for his superiors' approval later. Those men who received Stephens' orders carried them out, but they sometimes feared official reprimand. One worrier was Matthew Lewis, deputy secretary at war. Lewis pleaded that Ste-

[2] Lord Frederick North to William Eden, Aug. 22, 1775 (?): B.M., MSS Add. 34,412, f. 344.

[3] North habitually communicated to Stephens private pieces of intelligence for the admiralty, and Germain admitted that "the better care" might be taken of matters meriting admiralty attention were business done through Stephens. See, for example, P.R.O., Adm. 1/4287, and Lord George Germain to William Knox, Feb. 12, 1780: Knox Papers 5/27, Clements Library.

phens clear him of any impropriety in acting on the admiralty secretary's wishes:

> I ventured to send by express on Monday the orders which you represented to me as so necessary for carrying on the impress on the coasts of Kent & Sussex the end of this week, & I have now to request that an official letter may be sent to the secretary at war agreeable to the annexed draft, which will meet Mr. Jenkinson's ideas and justify me for the step I presumed to take without his immediate directions.[4]

In order to comply with this plea Stephens juggled the admiralty out-letter book. He dated the official missive requested by the deputy secretary July 19, although Lewis had not even asked for it until three days later.[5] Eight letters entered in the out-letter book before, and four entered after, the one of July 19 are dated July 24. Obviously then, Stephens drafted the command to Lewis July 24 and purposely dated it five days earlier in order to protect his colleague. In theory Stephens had chanced a reprimand for his falsification, but the secretary believed he had acted properly. He considered it part of his duty to insure the fleet its proper complement of men, so he shouldered responsibility and flouted routine procedure.

The navy profited from Stephens' semiofficial labors in other ways, as did the first lord of the admiralty who directed it. In his concern over the preparedness of Plymouth, Lord Sandwich told General Amherst

---

[4] Matthew Lewis to Philip Stephens, July 22, 1779: P.R.O., Adm. 1/4329.

[5] Philip Stephens to Charles Jenkinson, July 19, 1779: P.R.O., Adm. 2/563, p. 278. Stephens requested military assistance to reinforce the press gangs because there were not enough sailors available for this service.

where confidence could be placed. "I have written fully to Mr. Stephens upon the subject of the defence of Plymouth in consequence of a letter received at our office from the navy board." Again, he said: "If your lordship will send your secretary to morrow to Mr. Stephens, he will particularly explain to him all that has & can be done by us in this business."[6] Sandwich's action in 1781 further showed his reliance on his chief factotum. Admiral Darby, who commanded the western squadron, found to his grief that the united French and Spanish fleets had swept into the Channel. He appealed at once to Sandwich for reinforcements.[7] When the first lord received this disquieting news, he "immediately came to this place [Fulham] to settle with Mr. Stephens what information should be sent to Admiral Darby; for as to reinforcement to make him able to engage the enemy if they are really in these seas it is impracticable."[8] Stephens resided in Fulham, and Sandwich, instead of ordering the secretary to Whitehall for discussion, "Immediately came" to the secretary's house.

If the first lord needed Stephens to help plan naval defenses, he also relied upon the secretary to advise offensive strategy. Admiral George Rodney's brilliant relief of Gibraltar proved one of the most significant successes of the war—a maneuver which brought Rodney renewed public acclaim and enhanced his career. The *Sandwich Papers* reveal Secretary Stephens' part in drawing up plans for this relief. That part was significant, for

[6] Earl of Sandwich to Baron Amherst, July 11, 1779: P.R.O., War Office 34/116, ff. 87-88.

[7] George Darby to Earl of Sandwich, Aug. 17, 1781: *Sandwich Papers*, IV, 49.

[8] Earl of Sandwich to George III, Aug. 25, 1781: Sir John Fortescue, ed., *The Correspondence of King George the Third from 1760 to December 1783* (6 vols., London, 1927-1928), V, 267-268.

Sandwich only corrected a portion of Stephens' draft and added a last paragraph to the proposal.[9]

While Stephens drafted strategy, aided the press gangs, and cooperated with other men in assuring proper transportation, supply, and communication, he also prepared the defense of the Sandwich administration against parliamentary assaults by the opposition. During 1782, when the admiralty confronted its critics, Stephens proved more than an "extra commissioner," as "Spider" John Robinson[10] partially acknowledged in January. The treasury secretary called for a strategy meeting among the men who guided policy. One of those he suggested was Philip Stephens. "It will be right in my opinion," Robinson stated to Sandwich, "not only to have Lord Mulgrave present at the meeting on Saturday, but also all the other lords of the admiralty and Mr. Stephens; and so I mean to propose to Lord North unless you disapprove it."[11] Well might Stephens' presence be desired: he had prepared the information which Sandwich used and Mulgrave quoted nearly verbatim in defending the admiralty from its parliamentary detractors. The later debate in the Lords concerned the bungling which resulted in de Grasse's superiority at Chesapeake Bay during the Yorktown campaign. Sandwich orally elaborated upon Stephens' written draft of defense when he responded to his opponents in the House of Lords.[12] In the House of Commons Charles

9 See "Proposal for the relief of Gibraltar," *Sandwich Papers*, III, 186-187.

10 See Butterfield, *George III*, p. 119.

11 John Robinson to Earl of Sandwich, Jan. 24, 1782: *Sandwich Papers*, IV, 277.

12 The Duke of Chandos moved to censure the administration on March 6, 1782. Sandwich's reply may be found on pages 231-234 of John Debrett, ed., *The Parliamentary Register; a History of the*

James Fox moved four changes—which also included several minor indictments—against the admiralty. Stephens had anticipated every one of Fox's maneuvers and had prepared specific answers to each attack. Mulgrave, a junior lord of the admiralty, defended administration. In refuting Fox he followed Stephens' memorandum almost to the letter.[13]

If Stephens carried an unusually heavy burden at the admiralty, his colleagues at the treasury, Grey Cooper and John Robinson, also faced increased business. Robinson—best known for his parliamentary electioneering—worked unremittingly at the treasury to prosecute the war. Time and again he set an example of conscientious attention to duty. He sent Lord Hillsborough in 1780 a list of the provisions which the treasury proposed to ship in the convoy for Gibraltar and Minorca. He begged Hillsborough to approve the list quickly, for no ships could weigh anchor for the beleaguered garrisions without lists of specific articles and quantities of provisions in their cargoes.[14] But Robinson

---

Proceedings and Debates of the House of Lords . . . (45 vols., London, 1780-1796), VIII. Compare the reply to Stephens' memorandum in *Sandwich Papers*, IV, 344-349.

[13] Stephens listed thirty possible charges the opposition could make, and placed next to each charge a defense of administration. Fox moved four indictments against the admiralty: (1) de Grasse should have been prevented from sailing to the West Indies; (2) the St. Eustatius convoy should not have been lost; (3) the admiralty inexcusably failed to acknowledge that the combined fleets were in the Channel; and (4) the entire conduct of the Dutch war was bungled. Several minor points, included in these four charges, embraced eight of Stephens' "list of possibles." For Stephens' memorandum, see *Sandwich Papers*, IV, 315-344. Fox's motion is in *Parliamentary Register . . . House of Commons*, V, 406-412. Mulgrave's reply is on pages 412-415 of *ibid.*

[14] John Robinson to Earl of Hillsborough, Nov. 2, 1780: P.R.O., S.P. 37/26, f. 192.

did not let the matter rest here. He informed Undersecretary Stanier Porten that "the urgency of the Gibraltar and Minorca service becomes so pressing that you must excuse my earnest request that you will again lay before Lord Hillsborough the necessity of an immediate decision."[15] Robinson thus hastened to grease the creaky machinery for relieving Britain's most important Mediterranean base.

Robinson also attempted to smooth the operation of other parts of that machinery. He represented at great length to Philip Stephens in June of 1776 the impossibility of carrying on operations if admiralty regulations forbade the licensing of any ships transporting provisions to America that lacked specification of particular stores and provisions. Robinson deemed the matter so urgent that he wrote to his colleague before consulting First Lord North. The treasury secretary implied that Stephens could circumvent the admiralty requirement if he wished:

> But I hope you will allow me further to remark that while the objection is formally settling, which I own I think trivial, his Majesty's service is substantially suffering. Believe me it is no easy task, but an arduous business, to supply near 50,000 men at such a distance, with every necessary for their support, in the present situation of this country exhausted almost I may say of ships, which can be spared from its commerce and under many other disadvantages, and every accident that impedes, is greatly distressing and may be fatal.[16]

Stephens' colleague hoped that ships laden at Cork

[15] John Robinson to Sir Stanier Porten, Nov. 18, 1780: P.R.O., S.P. 37/26, f. 92.

[16] John Robinson to Philip Stephens, June 16, 1776: P.R.O., Adm. 1/4287.

would not be delayed for lack of an admiralty license which required particular specification of each ship's cargo.[17]

Robinson did not limit his efforts only to circumventing naval red tape. He also attended to other areas of administration. He wrote Undersecretary Porten in August of 1779 concerning the customs. In consequence of a conversation with North and Sandwich, Robinson noted, "I yesterday dispatched the orders respecting the revenue cutters to the respective boards in England and Scotland under whose direction they are in order that no time might be lost, tho' we had not received the official letter from you authorizing that measure."[18]

Grey Cooper also shared in the efforts of the British treasury during the American Revolution. Cooper, although involved in American affairs to a lesser extent than many of his colleagues, thought often about America. James Marriot, the king's advocate general, believed Cooper had great, if not the greatest, influence over North in regard to British war measures. He asked Cooper to discuss with North the capture of foreign vessels off the American coast and to draft a clear legal statement pertaining generally to seizure and condemnation of ships at sea. Marriot hoped Cooper would hand North the proposals at the *"first proper moment and when you can engage him to read them with you."* Marriot then aired other plans relative to the prosecution of the war. He deemed Cooper the only person fit to debate them with North, the only one possessing

---

[17] Unfortunately, Robinson's plan in this instance fell upon deaf ears. See Philip Stephens to John Robinson, June 19, 1776: P.R.O., Adm. 2/552, p. 168.

[18] John Robinson to Sir Stanier Porten, Aug. 20, 1770: P.R.O., S.P. 37/25, f. 199.

sufficient authority to see the proposals carried out.[19]

Whether or not Marriot overestimated Cooper's importance to North's war policy, the treasury secretary interested himself in some aspects of that policy. Supply —so necessary to an army—came under his scrutiny. It appears that on one occasion the secretary personally arranged with one Anthony Merry for supplying the army.[20] The negotiation of terms showed Cooper's concern for proper army supplies in America. Merry proposed to charter four ships, send them to Mogadore for oxen and sheep, and then transport the cattle to Boston or wherever the commander in chief in America would direct for the use of the army. Supposedly the merchant made his suggestions to the treasury, but the rough drafts of Cooper's letters reveal that the secretary probably discussed the matter with North alone, and that whatever terms were made, Cooper made them for North's approval. North and Cooper wished a contract for the operation, but Merry found several disadvantages in such a formal agreement. Finally the treasury authorized the merchant to provide the ships and cargoes on account of the government and to transport them as proposed. Of course he should prepare proper vouchers, letters, and copies of letters he would

[19] James Marriot to Grey Cooper, Feb. 15, 1775: P.R.O., T. 1/508, ff. 77-79.

[20] The series of correspondence relating to the arrangement is in P.R.O., T. 1/519, ff. 75-96. Many of these letters are rough drafts in Cooper's hand. Cooper might note he had Lord North's authority to tell Merry such and such a matter, and then cross out "Lord North" and substitute "treasury." Cooper wanted to make official the letter to Merry warning about ship hiring, but probably lacked official authorization. He therefore had to cross out, rewrite, and make the letter sound official without specifying its official character. The letters thus show the manner in which Cooper worked and the way treasury decisions were often reached.

write in the execution of the business. Merry could depend on a "regular and punctual payment" of the costs, and on completion of the venture a commission "adequate to the business done and the service performed by you for the public." Cooper's work yet remained unfinished. He warned Merry to stop hiring ships in the Thames at a higher price than normal. He found a man willing to insure the venture against all risks. Finally, he told Merry to deliver the supplies to Howe at Halifax, Nova Scotia, and informed Howe of the merchant's coming. The negotiations, begun in January of 1776, were completed in May. Cooper toiled hard throughout the affair, as the drafts of his letters reveal.

Cooper carried on other important labors at the treasury during the Revolution,[21] but subministerial collaboration rather than single-handed effort usually characterized the work of the minor men. Indeed, interdepartmental cooperation encompassed all matters from tactics to logistics. John Pownall and Philip Stephens, for example, were jointly important to the determination of a military matter in 1775. In October of that year Lord North mentioned to Pownall the possibility of sending an artillery company to Halifax, Nova Scotia. Such a company would reinforce a position believed vulnerable. Of course General Amherst, the former commander in chief in America, had to be consulted on the matter. But the latter did not decide on the troop movement until he had conversed with Secretary Pownall and Secretary Stephens. "Sir Jeffrey Amherst and Mr. Stephens," Pownall told King George after the conversation, "concurred with Mr. Pownall that it [the dispatching of the company] would be accompanied with very great haz-

[21] For instance, he personally handled the funds to cover the cost of transporting the Carlisle peace commissioners to America.

ard, so late in the year." North then changed his mind and decided not to order the movement until he had consulted the king.[22] Thus the opinion of two subministers governed the sending of troops to a vulnerable North American position.

Often the minor men overlooked the legal niceties that hindered swift execution of necessary business. Undersecretary Porten and Secretary Robinson jointly moved an important operation without waiting for official authority. "I am this instant got home from Ld. North at Bushy Park," Robinson told his colleague, "where he is arrived perfectly well. On my coming hither only I have found your letter and it is now too late to send it & the inclosure to Lord North." But Porten could "assure Lord Weymouth that I will not fail to lay the paper before Lord North tomorrow morning, and if he agrees in opinion with Ld. Weymouth which I have no doubt he will do, the necessary orders shall be immediately sent to the customs, and we will put the business afterwards in an *official train*."[23] Robinson and either Porten or Undersecretary Fraser in 1779 again avoided technicalities for the sake of efficiency. Robinson sent Mr. Green, a former smuggler who now sailed the Channel for British intelligence, to Stephens at the admiralty. Green had "serviceable propositions." But since the ex-smuggler sought a pardon for the murder of one Thomas Cole in 1759, Robinson urged him to visit an undersecretary in order to bargain for his amnesty from Secretary of State Weymouth. Green, after all, was useful to the war effort. Undersecretary Fraser or Porten replied that Green could not be pardoned for the murder, since he had only

[22] John Pownall to George III, Oct. 19, 1775: *Geo. III Corr.*, III, 272.

[23] John Robinson to Sir Stanier Porten, Sept. 16, 1777: P.R.O., S.P. 37/23, f. 262.

been indicted and had managed to escape before trial. Furthermore, it appeared that Green actually delivered the blow that killed Cole, although a man present but not actually participating had been tried and executed for the murder. "But," the undersecretary hastened to add, "as Green has rendered some meritorious service of late to government, might it not be more proper to give him some pecuniary reward to enable him and his family to live more comfortably in some foreign country."[24] The subministers knew how to deal with men.

In spite of their willingness to coordinate their efforts, their intelligence, and their administrative shrewdness, minor men sometimes blundered. A series of mistakes by various departments in 1779 resulted in the French being supplied with copper contrary to the wishes of the admiralty. The admiralty lords informed Secretary of State Weymouth on September 18 that they knew of orders in London for sending to France by way of Ostend twenty thousand sheets of copper sheathing for the French navy. Weymouth ordered Porten to pass the information on to John Robinson and to request that Robinson place the matter before the treasury. Steps could be "immediately taken" to prevent the metal's export, since it was of "utmost consequence to defeat the means of sheathing the enemy's fleet with copper."[25] On September 22 Robinson told Porten surprising news. The treasury secretary had originally transmitted the intelligence of the copper sheathing to the admiralty, because the treasury lacked authority to stop its being shipped abroad. It could only delay the sailing. The treasury had

[24] John Robinson to an undersecretary of state, July 12, 1779: P.R.O., S.P. 37/13, f. 112, and Sir Stanier Porten or William Fraser to John Robinson, no date: *Ibid.*, f. 334.

[25] Sir Stanier Porten to John Robinson, Sept. 18, 1779: P.R.O., S.P. 37/25, f. 260.

ordered the customs commissioners to effect the delay, but Robinson believed an embargo on copper sheathing the only permanent solution. He had talked with Lord North and Lord Sandwich, who had both approved such a step. Now Robinson wished to ascertain through Porten whether Weymouth would also agree. If he did, then Lord Gower's permission must be sought. Sandwich, meanwhile, agitated for immediate embargo.[26] Such delays, procrastination, and interoffice exchanges culminated in disaster. Customs Secretary Stanley informed Robinson on September 23 that the object of their worries had already sailed from England with seventeen tons of copper and was probably in Ostend. Stanley had done his best, but he had no legal authority to impede its departure longer.[27] Thus occurred an incredible blunder, but a blunder which owed as much to the ministers as to the subministers. Robinson had first discovered the matter and in good faith informed the admiralty. From there it had been ineffectively tossed from department to department. But the fault also lay with the admiralty, customs, and treasury secretaries, and with the undersecretary of state. Had they acted as they so often did, had they circumvented official channels, the sheathing might not have found its way to the bottoms of French ships.

Yet for every failure to prevent exportation of goods which might help the enemy's war effort, the subministers counted several successes. Vigilant efforts often thwarted the exportation of gunpowder and arms. In the autumn of 1775 John Pownall told John Robinson

26 John Robinson to Sir Stanier Porten, Sept. 22, 1779: P.R.O., S.P. 37/25, f. 266.
27 Edward Stanley to John Robinson, Aug. 16, 1775: P.R.O., S.P. 37/25, f. 270.

of a traffic in arms from London to North America. Pownall's department thought the stationing of a naval ship
in the Downs and another in the five fathom channel
would protect customs officers and facilitate the searching of vessels outward bound with contraband. Pownall himself wished for two or three customs cutters
or sloops to cooperate with the naval vessels and examine ships cruising from the Downs to Gravesend. Dartmouth approved Pownall's idea and authorized Robinson to order the customs commissioners to station customs ships accordingly.[28] Robinson set to work immediately. He wrote to the revenue board, enclosed Pownall's
letter, and asserted that he was "directed to desire that
you will with all possible dispatch give the necessary
directions for this service accordingly."[29] William How
(or Howe), acting as secretary during Stanley's absence,
soon informed Robinson that the orders had been carried out.[30]

Four days after the undersecretary–treasury secretary–
customs interchange, Pownall again wrote to Robinson.
"I think it my duty in the absence of Lord Dartmouth
to acquaint you for the information of the lords commissioners of the treasury" of a project to transport gunpowder from London to Africa. Pownall suspected the
whole business. The gunpowder was being sent on account of a person who had not long ago "applied both
to you and to me for a license to ship 100 barrels and
was told he could not have it." Nevertheless the same

[28] John Pownall to John Robinson, Aug. 16, 1775: P.R.O., C.O.
5/146, ff. 27-28.
[29] John Robinson to John Pownall, Aug. 17, 1775: P.R.O., C.O.
5/146, f. 29; and John Robinson to the customs commissioners, Aug.
17, 1775: *Ibid.*, f. 31.
[30] William How to John Robinson, Aug. 18, 1775: C.O. 5/146, ff.
35-36.

man acquired official permission through other channels. Now he intended to send near double his initial estimate, much more powder than the trade warranted.[31] Robinson wasted no time. He too thought the matter sufficiently important to justify sidestepping red tape. The treasury secretary told his customs counterpart to stop the suspected ship immediately. The latter should issue the necessary orders on his own initiative if the customs board were not sitting.[32] The acting customs secretary complied promptly. Customs officers at Deal then uncovered not one but two vessels loaded with excess gunpowder and lightened them by 100 barrels of explosive.[33]

One search, however, failed to end the matter. The customs commissioners now alerted themselves to their full responsibilities. Further probing revealed many ships with unauthorized powder perhaps destined for rebel muskets. It also uncovered a wily smuggling trick. Often those skippers earnest for an American victory ballasted their vessels with flint, so indispensable to most eighteenth-century weapons.[34]

Contraband also included more than copper, gunpowder, and flint. The British government could not allow secret intelligence and potential rebel officers to leave England. John Robinson told John Pownall of the "Rev. Mr. Maddison of William & Mary" who had ob-

[31] John Pownall to John Robinson, Aug. 21, 1775: P.R.O., C.O. 5/146, f. 37.

[32] John Robinson to William How, Aug. 21, 1775: P.R.O., C.O. 5/146, f. 41.

[33] Collector and comptroller at Deal to customs secretary, Aug. 22, 1775: P.R.O., C.O. 5/146, f. 47; William How to John Robinson, Aug. 23, 1775: *Ibid.*, f. 45; and collector and comptroller at Deal to the customs commissioners, Aug. 29, 1775: *Ibid.*, f. 95.

[34] Edward Stanley to John Robinson, Sept. 15, 1775: P.R.O., C.O. 5/146, f. 117.

tained permission in 1776 to return to America. The
pastor carried in his shirts, in the lining of his clothes,
and in his baggage treasonable correspondence. The
affair suggested that American spies in Britain wrote
what they wished in anticipation that Maddison (and
men of his profession?) would never be searched.[35] Pownall could now close this loophole. On another occasion
the treasury secretary informed his colleague of several
American ship captains preparing to embark for North
America solely to enlist their services against the mother
country.[36]

The American Undersecretary in turn informed Robinson constantly of matters within the latter's jurisdiction. One of Pownall's hirelings mentioned a ship in the
Thames, with American passengers aboard, that awaited
secret dispatches. Pownall passed the news on to Robinson. The treasury secretary thought that orders should
come from Germain expressing "His Majesty's pleasure"
to seize the vessel. But the urgency of the situation admitted no loss of time, and Robinson issued necessary orders
for the ship's papers to be examined.[37]

Prevention of illegal activity often depended upon
knowledge of it coming to the subministers by way of
informers. One minor man, Undersecretary William
Eden, directed an "argus-eyed" secret service whose network of agents embraced most of Europe. His colleagues
also used men to report enemy movements and intrigue.
John Pownall maintained intelligence agents who sup-

[35] John Robinson to John Pownall, May 9, 1776: P.R.O., C.O.
5/147, f. 260.

[36] John Robinson to John Pownall, Dec. 8, 1775: P.R.O., C.O.
5/146, f. 273.

[37] For the intricate series of correspondence relating to this matter,
see P.R.O., C.O. 5/146, ff. 207-239.

plied him with accounts of French action before France entered the American Revolution in support of the United States.[38] Edward Stanley often forwarded William Knox data concerning American-French trade and the activities of privateers.[39] John Robinson sent Knox messages about troop movements in America and French military plans.[40] The subministers constantly exchanged communications on enemy fleet operations in America; on doings in the Netherlands, in France, and in Spain; on clandestine meetings among American spies in London; and many other matters.[41] The secretaries and undersecretaries were mines of information, and Britain's inability to coordinate her military operations resulted not from lack of information concerning enemy movements and intentions.

Indeed, Britain's failure owed more to poor officers and to breakdowns in communication, transportation, and supply than to scanty information concerning the enemy. The subministers could do little about poor officers, but they strove mightily to overcome the other difficulties. Undersecretary Stanier Porten once acted in the absence of his superior to maintain communications with Gibraltar. He informed Anthony Todd, secretary to the post office, of French capture of a sloop carrying important dispatches to the Mediterranean bastion from the admiralty and the secretary of state's

[38] See for example Edward Bridgen to John Pownall, July 27, 1775: P.R.O., C.O. 5/154, f. 163.

[39] Edward Stanley to William Knox, Sept. 17, 1776: P.R.O., C.O. 5/148, f. 223; and Edward Stanley to William Knox, June 21, 1777: P.R.O., C.O. 5/149, f. 467.

[40] John Robinson to William Knox, Sept. 10, 1780: P.R.O., C.O. 5/152, f. 230.

[41] This type of interdepartmental correspondence was carried on incessantly. For more instances, see P.R.O., C.O. 5/138, ff. 98-184.

office. The information in those dispatches had to reach "the Rock" immediately. Only a Captain Burnaby, leaving Falmouth in his packet for Gibraltar via Lisbon could depart at once with the messages. "After stating to you these circumstances" Porten told Todd, "I must leave you to do what is most proper for the publick service, and can only express my wish that you must think it advisable to send Captain Burnaby directly from Falmouth to Gibraltar with the despatches that will be sent to you from this office to morrow for Gibraltar."[42] Todd probably did his best for the fortress's mail, for he had always cooperated with the state departments. Indeed, he took particular pains to post to the American undersecretary packet-boat schedules well in advance of expected departures.[43]

Other communication problems also demanded constant consideration. When Undersecretary Knox thought that customs officers unnecessarily delayed messengers with important dispatches from America to Whitehall, he asked the customs secretary to correct the situation. He also suggested new customs practice to deal with messengers in the future.[44] When Knox wished a packet to sail immediately with important mail he promptly requested Todd to take the necessary steps.[45] When the treasury had important letters to send or North had personal commands to dispatch, Secretary Robinson

[42] Sir Stanier Porten to Anthony Todd, Oct. 12, 1778: P.R.O., S.P. 37/12, f. 300.

[43] Anthony Todd to William Knox, Mar. 4, 1780: P.R.O., C.O. 5/137, f. 130.

[44] Stanley followed Knox's suggestion. See William How to William Knox, Aug. 18, 1777: P.R.O., C.O. 5/149, f. 487; and Edward Stanley to William Knox, Aug. 19, 1777: *Ibid.*, f. 491.

[45] William Knox to Anthony Todd, Aug. 4, 1777: P.R.O., C.O. 5/136, f. 50.

171

speedily saw them aboard the proper packet boats.[46] When Secretary Philip Stephens discovered information relative to enemy fleet movements he sent it without waste of time to Lord North. He further prodded slow departments with the reminder that "the departure of the sloop depends upon your dispatches."[47] The American undersecretaries of state and the secretary to the post office often worked out between themselves, without consulting their superiors, many of the other myriad details of proper communication.[48]

Supply, no less than communication, demanded the attention of the subministers. One item for the army in America—horses—illustrates well the complexities of supply. Evidently an army colonel had acquainted the ordnance board with his hope of purchasing 700 horses and had requested 12,000 horseshoes for them. Another colonel then suggested that the ordnance board should forge an additional 20,000 horseshoes for the animals going to America instead of waiting until they arrived there with hopes that some loyal American blacksmiths would offer their services. The ordnance board, however, notoriously independent, needed urging from the American department if it was to provide a large supply of horseshoes. Robinson, a treasury secretary, did not wish to antagonize either the head of the American department, Lord George Germain, or the ordnance board by writing

[46] John Robinson to William Knox, Jan. 5, 1778: P.R.O., C.O. 5/150, f. 9.

[47] Philip Stephens to Thomas De Grey, Sept. 28, 1779: Germain Papers, fol. 10, Clements Library.

[48] P.R.O., C.O. 5/136 is filled with correspondence between the post office and the American department regarding packet boats. Ff. 3, 7, 9, and 17 show the complicated problems of operating a competent mail service. The difficulty of finding able seamen to serve in mail boats was only one of the problems which plagued the departments.

directly to them telling them their business. Yet he favored the plan of shipping the shoes from England to America instead of depending on an uncertain supply there. He therefore hoped a judicious word to Pownall, who as undersecretary to Germain had his chief's confidence, would prompt the American department to write an official request to ordnance for the necessary horseshoes. In an entirely roundabout fashion the treasury secretary had hit upon a scheme for furnishing an essential item, although responsibility in the area rested with a department of government different from the one Robinson served.[49]

Interwoven with supply was transportation. The many goods Britain stockpiled at home or in Ireland for the army served no purpose unless serviceable vessels transported them to America when needed. Faulty, excessively slow transportation invited disaster, and the secretaries and undersecretaries struggled to overcome the entangled system that encouraged delay. When Secretary of State Germain worried over the admiralty's providing a convoy for transports carrying reinforcements to the Leeward Islands, for example, he urged his undersecretary to straighten out the matter with Philip Stephens.[50] When William Knox deemed urgent the sending transports from Germany to America without loss of time he wrote Undersecretary Fraser to see what could be done. Fraser promised support. "I will speak to Lord Stormont upon it," Fraser told his colleague, "& if you will talk to Lord George, & Lord Amherst should also be consulted; if they think it right we may see what

[49] John Robinson to John Pownall, Jan. 11, 1776: P.R.O., T. 1/522, f. 166.

[50] Lord George Germain to William Knox, Feb. 12, 1780: Knox Papers 5/27.

can be done at the Admty."[51] Fraser's direct approach to the matter echoed the countless endeavors of other subministers to provide proper transportation.

Problems of transportation, communication, and supply, however, were only a few of the difficulties that taxed all the subministerial resources. Minor men seemed always to be involved in all phases of the war effort. Sometimes they corresponded with one another in the official, stilted form for interdepartmental business. In these instances they may or may not have acted under the authority of their superiors, although the official form stipulated they had so acted. Frequently they acknowledged that they pursued a particular course on their own initiative because their chiefs were absent. Often they exchanged informal notes of their own ideas and plans. But on their own or working under orders the secretaries and undersecretaries forged a vital link in the chain of administrative command. They possessed the initiative, the ability, and the efficiency to ensure that administration functioned despite obstacles that threatened to break it down.

Great Britain lost the American colonies. Perhaps that loss may in part be attributed to subministerial work. The subministers, however, offered up their best against the inertia of the ponderous machinery of the eighteenth century. For all their influence on administration, they could not appoint the commanding generals or admirals in America, nor could they supervise grand strategy.

[51] William Fraser to William Knox, Mar. 18, 1781: P.R.O., C.O. 5/144, f. 17.

CHAPTER SIX

Ironic Aftermath

As THE American Revolution dragged to a close, two of the most influential subministers, former Undersecretaries John Pownall and William Knox, faced the ironic climax of their careers. Of the two, Pownall had prospered better materially and had retained little bitterness toward the former American colonies. By the end of 1782 he had been drinking from his "cup of comfort" for six years as a commissioner of excise. He had shed his arduous burdens as an undersecretary of state in 1776 and also whatever animosity he may have felt toward America. Now, six years later, he prepared to aid Lord Shelburne in effecting a commercial reconciliation between Britain and the United States. Knox, on the other hand, seemed to find the new nation an unwelcome intruder into the family of sovereign powers. He had lost his position as undersecretary upon abolition of the American department in 1782, and as a consequence he had lost a fine income. He had watched Britain flouted and beaten. He had further suffered the humiliation of seeing the Earl of Shelburne, a minister he heartily disliked, once more returned to power. Knox, unlike the noble lord, wished to exclude the United States from any commercial concessions in the British Empire. Thus stood in 1782 two former undersecretaries, firm friends, who had worked together so closely in the past.

First Lord of the Treasury Shelburne wished to provide for reciprocal trade with the United States in the preliminary articles of peace, and he turned to his board of trade secretary of many years ago, John Pownall, for advice and consultation. Pownall eagerly cooperated, for he had always believed the British West Indies depended for survival upon unbroken trade with America. In January of 1783 the former undersecretary sent to Shelburne a report on British-American commercial relations. It suggested parliamentary legislation to exempt the United States from the trade laws applied to other nations, and it deemed expedient revision of the laws which granted bounties on naval stores, rice, indigo, and other commodities.[1] Pownall next talked privately with the first lord. After this conversation Pownall submitted to him the draft for a parliamentary bill regulating trade between Britain and the United States. The draft recognized the United States as an independent sovereign power, proposed free trade with the new nation, and exempted America from the restrictions imposed on alien commerce. It further provided that trade should be regulated by orders in council "for such reciprocal privileges and exemptions to the subjects of both nations in their mutual commerce & intercourse . . . on the solid ground of just reciprocity."[2]

The Fox-North coalition, however, did not wish "just reciprocity," and it replaced Shelburne's government in April of 1783. The earl had introduced some measures into the House of Commons corresponding to Pownall's suggestions,[3] but the coalition opposed reciprocal trade. After taking power it pushed its own measures through Parliament. On May 8 Commons passed a bill which called for trade regulation by orders in council. North,

[1] John Pownall to Earl of Shelburne, Jan. 30, 1783: Shelburne Papers 72/471-484.

[2] John Pownall to Earl of Shelburne, Feb. 7, 1783: Shelburne Papers 72/507-513.

[3] The various proposals Shelburne introduced and the subsequent changes they underwent may be followed in *Bill and Acts for Provisional Trade and Intercourse with the United States* (London, 1783-1784).

however, intended to use orders to restrict rather than to expand British West Indian–American commerce.[4] He sent his son and heir, George Augustus North, to William Knox. The emissary first asked Pownall's former colleague to draft an act of Parliament for regulating trade between "our remaining colonies, our West India islands & the United States." Knox explained what Lord North already knew, that an order in council could effect the desired purpose, and he asked George Augustus if his father would prefer instead the draft of an order in council. North so desired, and Knox set to work.

His labors resulted in the order in council of July 2, 1783, which forbade imports into the West Indies of ships stores, timber, livestock, live provisions, and all species of grain by any save British subjects in British ships manned by British citizens. Knox certainly believed the order would restrict exchange between America and the West Indies, and he considered his work a triumph. Men of similar persuasion concurred. The Earl of Sheffield found "sincere pleasure" in seeing the order "passed exactly" as Knox had drawn it.[5] Although the now for-

[4] Fox had actually proposed on Apr. 2 a bill allowing the king to regulate trade by orders in council for six months. The Lords amended the bill and extended the time limit to Dec. 27. Fox then stipulated the Commons could not accept amendments to what he deemed a money bill, but he immediately introduced a new bill embodying the Lords' proposals. The measure passed the Commons on May 8, the day Fox proposed it. See *Parliamentary Register*, x, 1-2. The Lords assented to the bill on May 12, and the king signed it on the same day. The statute, 23 Geo. III, c. 39, par. 3, was renewed from time to time.

[5] Earl of Sheffield to William Knox, July 4, 1783: Knox Papers 7/8. Knox later stated, probably in all honesty, that he feared American-West Indian commerce would injure British navigation. See "William Knox: Evidence before the Committee of Trade, 18 March 1784," in Vincent Harlow and Frederick Madden, *British Colonial Developments, 1774-1834, Select Documents* (Oxford, 1955), pp. 260-263.

CONCLUSION

The Subministers, A New Dimension

NOT many of the eighteenth-century subministers have stirred significant historical interest. A few individuals, such as John Robinson and Charles Jenkinson, have received considerable attention, but the subministers as a group have been largely neglected. Sir Lewis Namier pointed to them as civil servants in his *Structure of Politics,* but he gave them only passing attention in a work devoted to greater problems. They of course figure in many of the post-Namier political histories of eighteenth-century England. But again the subministers act only minor parts in the historiographic panorama of power, politics, and patronage. The political historians concentrate, rightly, on their political rather than their administrative role.

Their administrative work cannot, however, be neglected. Eighteenth-century administrative historians see the subministerial hand in many departmental policies. But like political historians, they necessarily center on their particular area of interest. The result of such concentration provides at best only a blurred picture of the "civil servants."

Admittedly, formidable difficulties face anyone who wishes to bring the blurred picture into focus. So many problems—the number of men holding government positions, their exact powers, their relations with superiors, their impact on policy—face the investigator. Perhaps the civil servants can be studied only one at a time, but someone must start the process. The subministers are too important to the eighteenth century to remain in darkness.

179

More intensive study of their work would assuredly clarify the history of the entire English civil service. That organization did not begin all at once with the introduction of competitive examinations in the nineteenth century. No institution emerges from a vacuum. Victorian reformers railed at the sinecures, the corruption, and the favoritism of eighteenth-century public office. These evils existed, but they did not exist to the same degree in all departments, and they touched some men far less than others. An admiralty secretary cannot be compared to a clerk of the pells or a master of the revels in Ireland, so much is obvious. But he cannot properly even be compared to a treasury secretary, or at least dismissed as an official who fulfilled a similar political and administrative purpose. Despite the comparable work performed by each man for his respective department, the admiralty accorded permanent tenure and a "civil servant" status to its secretary. The treasury denied both to its subordinate. Eighteenth-century parliamentary investigators recognized the distinction between the admiralty and the treasury. In the admiralty and in a few other offices with similar traditions, a practice grew that must have contributed to the Victorian conception of the civil service. Only careful investigation, however, can distinguish clearly the civil servant from the placeman or the politician.

If insufficient study or lack of evidence, or both, deny satisfactory definitions, the demonstrable role of the subministers in the American Revolution ought to add a new dimension to interpretations of that movement and, perhaps, help reconcile some contradictory views concerning it. To the first eloquent chroniclers of the Revolution the issues were clear and involved only a few subministers in an unconstitutional cabal. The

A New Dimension

Whig interpretation declared the Tory ministries from 1763 to 1775 arbitrary and tyrannical. The leading Tories, a party that George III had reelevated to power, conceived and passed American measures consonant with their absolutist convictions. The subministers, however, were not an administrative element to execute Tory designs, but rather a group of "king's friends." They held seats in Parliament, places, and pensions by grace of the monarch. They voted on parliamentary American bills according to his personal whims, even if those whims ran contrary to the intentions of the occasional Whig ministers who held power. Some "king's friends," the Whigs averred, such as Charles Jenkinson, enjoyed a "secret" and "unconstitutional" influence over the monarch. "Backstairs intrigue" enabled them to whisper to George III about American policy as well as other measures without ever bothering to consult the officials in power. The third Hanoverian might usher his "king's friends" to his closet periodically for counsel and guidance and follow their opinions even if they ran entirely contrary to his cabinet's. Indeed, if circumstances occasionally forced the Crown to accept an unpalatable Whig cabinet, such as the Rockingham government of 1765, George used not only the "king's friends" opinions but their parliamentary votes to oust his enemies as soon as he had lined up suitable replacements. "King's friends" thus served America badly by helping the monarchy to rid itself of the only ministers friendly to the colonies. But whether they advised the king badly or voted in Parliament badly, the subministers were not an important administrative group who might influence policy directly and without political bias. The Whigs credited the most important "Tories"—George Grenville, Charles Townshend, and Lord North—with

North, Egremont, Shelburne, Germain, Sandwich, Rockingham, Chatham—these were the men, Whig and Tory,
who directed British energies from 1763 to 1783. The
subministerial role was secondary or even tertiary. Namier and historians writing in his tradition have lifted
the minor men from the shadows but label them all
"civil servants." Admittedly this gives the subministers
a new stature, but poses as many questions as it answers.
Many minor men were obviously not civil servants
or even forerunners of them. More importantly, the
political historians rarely examine at length the administration those civil servants were supposed to serve.
Instead they concentrate on the subministerial role in
politics. If the post-Namier historians consider American policy at all, which they rarely do at length, they
omit the subministerial role in that policy. The most
recent work from this school, Namier and Brooke's
Charles Townshend, devotes only a few pages to the
Townshend Duties and none at all to the customs commissioners who were nearly as important to them as the
Townshend himself.

But neither the chancellor of the exchequer nor many
of his colleagues before and after 1767 stand in a very
favorable light. The Namierites reject the old Whig
notion of "all Whigs good, all Tories bad." They substitute for it "no parties, no Whigs, no Tories, but factions
of politicians interested chiefly in local business, patronage, and office." Political historians have demonstrated fairly conclusively that ideology played little part
in the fights of the 1760's and 1770's among the various
factions. British politicians were locally-minded, and
getting into office was much more to the point than
what should be done once there. Ministers who thought
chiefly about turnpikes in Yorkshire and sinecures for

friends and relations, however, could be neither the
imperially-minded statesmen who lost half a continent
because of a point of view too broad nor the good Whigs
and bad Tories, with proper and improper ideals, who
lost America because evil temporarily triumphed over
virtue on the coattails of a king with absolutist intentions.

Perhaps good men, bad men, Whigs, Tories, imperialists, politicians, jumble together in the interpretations
of the Revolution because subministers have not hitherto been interjected to separate them. The minor men
might join the irreconcilables—Whig, imperial, modern,
political—together if they are given their share in the
British government of the revolutionary era. The pre-
ceding pages have attempted to show they do, indeed,
deserve a large share. In one way or another they participated in every major piece of legislation to emerge
during the era. Suppose Grenville was more interested
in general warrants, cider taxes, smuggling, and patronage than in American policy. He nonetheless had subministerial help capable of executing his vague American
plans. Some of it may have been as uninformed about
America as the Whigs liked to think Grenville was—
Whately, for example. But some subministers were vastly
experienced in American affairs. Men such as John Pownall assuredly fit the imperial idea. Similar circumstances apply to the other ministers and the American
programs associated with them.

Subministers either suggested, formulated, or implemented the Proclamation of 1763, the Sugar and Stamp
acts, Townshend Duties, American customs board,
Quebec Act, and Boston Port Bill. The powers they
enjoyed in office—staff supervision, management of correspondence, preparation of agendas—assured that they

would do so. The administratively oriented men—Edward Hooper, John Pownall, Philip Stephens—eschewed politics and placed the good of the service and the interests of empire over petty localisms. The politically oriented men—Thomas Whately, Maurice Morgann, Grey Cooper (for a period)—put politics and the political interests of their superiors above the particular job they happened to hold in administration. They, too, helped formulate American policy. Some of the subministers, such as William Wood, would have been "good" from a Whig point of view, and some, such as Whately, "bad." Some of them, such as Philip Stephens, were indeed the "civil servants" of the Namierites, civil servants who resembled closely their modern counterparts. Others, such as Charles Jenkinson, were the "king's friends" of the Whigs. The subministers had as many sides as historians have given to Whigs, Tories, administrators, and imperialists. These sides complemented each other from 1763 through 1783 to produce an American policy and an American war.

APPENDIX A

The Ghost of Thomas Whately

AFTER he left the treasury with his chief, George Grenville, Thomas Whately opened a momentous correspondence with Thomas Hutchinson, lieutenant governor of Massachusetts, and Andrew Oliver, secretary to the
province. The letters—somewhat informal since Oliver
was a friend of the family and Hutchinson an official
whom Whately respected highly—concerned public matters in the Bay Colony. Hutchinson and Oliver deemed
conditions there deplorable and constantly described to
their correspondent instances of anarchy and widespread
disloyalty to the British government.[1] The letters, although sometimes violent in tone, were private opinions of public officials not public reports. They were
written between 1767 and 1769, when Whately was
no longer secretary to the treasury but only a "man of
business" for a prominent opposition leader. Yet the
letters never remained in the obscurity intended by
their writers, although the correspondence was never
revealed to the public during Whately's life.

Whately did not, however, live many years after 1769.
When Grenville died in 1770 the former treasury secretary led the Grenville party back into the government.
Whately became a commissioner of trade in January of
1771 and, in June of the same year, an undersecretary of state for the northern department. Death claimed
the loyal Grenvillite one year later on May 26,
1772. Since Whately died unmarried and intestate, his
brother William, a prominent banker, administered his

1 The letters and other sources relative to them are in *Franklin
Before the Privy Council* (Boston, 1865).

effects. These effects included the Hutchinson-Oliver correspondence. By some method Benjamin Franklin secured this correspondence and sent it back to Massachusetts. He pleaded that the letters be kept from the public, but he might just as well have asked a combat-hardened infantryman not to fire at a charging enemy. Bostonians hated Oliver and Hutchinson, and when Sam Adams acquired the correspondence, Hutchinson's usefulness as a representative of the British authority diminished considerably. Adams read the damning epistles to the Massachusetts assembly, whose members immediately became incensed at their already-disliked chief executive. Hutchinson and Oliver—by now governor and lieutenant governor respectively—had committed "treason" against the Bay Colony. The assembly petitioned for their swift removal.[2] Thus the letters of the deceased Thomas Whately added to the grievances of the Massachusetts patriots against the British government. They also, finally, brought even greater consequences.

William Whately believed that his brother's old friend John Temple, who had borrowed some of Thomas's letters, had encouraged public revelation of their contents. He became so incensed at what he considered perfidious conduct that he fought a pistol duel with Temple. Then Benjamin Franklin assumed responsibility for the letters. In so doing, Franklin unwittingly sentenced himself to one of the most mortifying days of his life. One of his duties as agent for Massachusetts was to plead before the privy council the Bay Colony's petition to dismiss Hutchinson and Oliver. But the agent would face Solicitor General Alexander Wedderburn, who had been employed to act for the threatened officials. During

[2] The assembly's petition is in *Franklin*.

the privy council proceedings that followed Wedderburn heaped abuse on Franklin for opening private letters to public scrutiny. Angered and embarrassed, Franklin hardened his determination to oppose British colonial policy.[3]

Undoubtedly Franklin did not deserve Wedderburn's harangue, but Wedderburn does not deserve some of the calumny heaped upon him subsequently for his part in the affair. The incident has been described as a deliberate effort by the North ministry to "get" Franklin and teach the colonies manners.[4] This interpretation overlooks or discredits a statement of the solicitor general at the time of the hearing, that he felt deeply, personally attached to the memory of Whately. There seems little reason to doubt Wedderburn's sincerity, for the *Grenville Papers* testify to his close friendship with the former secretary. They often exchanged political gossip, visited each other's residence frequently, and acquired an intimate knowledge of each other's affairs. On one occasion Wedderburn cited Whately as a witness to his work before going on judicial circuit, and on a different occasion Whately claimed Wedderburn as one of his closest friends, and the only one he could visit at the particular time without taking long trips into the country.[5] Wedderburn may not have exemplified political virtue, and a political "deal" may have figured in his attack on Franklin. But he scarcely merits censure

[3] Parts of Wedderburn's speech are in *Franklin.*

[4] Carl Van Doren, in his *Benjamin Franklin* (New York, 1952), pp. 444-478, details the entire affair. He concludes that Wedderburn attacked Franklin not from personal animosity but in accordance with a plan concocted by the North ministry.

[5] For these exchanges, see Thomas Whately to George Grenville, June 13, 1776, and Alexander Wedderburn to George Grenville, July 9, 1766: *Grenville Papers*, III, 246-247, 261. See Thomas Whately to Charles Jenkinson, Sept. 18, 1766: *Jenkinson Papers*, p. 432.

for attacking the man he honestly believed aired the private correspondence of a dead friend in order to discredit an able official in a particularly troublesome part of the British empire.

Thus the ghost of Thomas Whately trod across the stage of British-colonial relations, embroiling people in duels, embarrassing a Massachusetts agent, harassing a Massachusetts governor, and inflaming Massachusetts opinion. The onetime treasury secretary, board of trade commissioner, undersecretary of state, amateur gardener, and Shakespearean critic found no peace even in death. Few colonists ever vented their wrath against Whately during his lifetime, because few men knew of his importance. Yet he, along with other "subministers," bore a major share of responsibility for American policy. His career ultimately proved doubly ironic. On the basis of letters from a lieutenant governor of Massachusetts to an ex-treasury secretary, the Bay Colony tried to remove Governor Hutchinson. This same Governor Hutchinson in 1771 found it necessary to insert a suitable name for a new Massachusetts town in its blank draft of incorporation. Hutchinson chose the name Whately.[6]

6 J. H. Temple, *History of the Town of Whately, Massachusetts* (Boston, 1872), pp. 82, 86.

The Mystery of the Stamp Act

ALTHOUGH subministers attempted to iron out the many wrinkles in the Stamp Act, neither they nor the ministry ever envisioned the problems it would create. The student who examines the several administrative sides to this "internal" tax concludes, from his own confusion, that the ministry itself must have been confused. For example, the number, duties, and pay of personnel connected with the act, the appointment of American officers, and the apportionment of stamps between America and the West Indies were never worked out before the stamp bill became the Stamp Act. Even legal procedures for enforcing the measure were not firmly established before the bill became law. Grenville, seemingly, was unsure of legal implications when the House of Commons committee of the whole house reported the stamp bill, February 7, 1765. He apparently asked former Attorney General Charles Yorke to consider the bill around this time, for Yorke submitted a detailed report to him on the measure ten days later. The former Crown lawyer found several defects. He considered the breviate too "short & defective." The measure stated imperfectly the offences which brought penalties and the method of recovering these penalties. Furthermore, Yorke believed that more extensive study might reveal that the only offences for which penalties could be laid would relate to counterfeiting of stamps, and these penalties could be enforced by anyone interested in the validity of the instruments and law proceedings to be stamped. If that were the case, could not ordinary courts of record in the colonies be entrusted with jurisdiction? Yorke considered American vice-admiralty courts "paultry & corrupt," and averred that the concurrent jurisdiction of the vice-admiralty court at Halifax "tho' respectible," was far away. "The stamp duties have nothing of a maritime or commercial nature," Yorke noted. "The precedent may, in argument, be extended far, to other future taxes, upon the colonies." Yet the former attorney general avoided the decision of whether the recovery of penalties should be left to a court of record, to two or three of the council in each colony appointed by the king, or to a judge of vice-admiralty.[1] Thus, while the stamp bill was on the floor of Commons, doubt still existed regarding the legal court for recovering penalties under the act, and what penalties could be recovered.

Perhaps such confusion surrounded plans for administration of the Stamp Act because the ministry was unsure of what it had passed. Whately informed Grenville on April 11, 1765: "I shall have the English stamp bill compleatly ready by your return. The American bill will I believe be in equal forwardness, & a clause will be prepared for your consideration concerning the fees of custom house officers."[2] Apparently Whately referred to an American stamp bill, yet Whately's American stamp bill had already been approved by the treasury in December of 1764 and the Stamp Act had been passed in March. Such failure to foresee contingencies might indicate, despite Edmund Morgan's argu-

---

[1] Charles Yorke to George Grenville, Feb. 17, 1765: Murray—Grenville Papers, Grenville B 4 file.

[2] Thomas Whately to George Grenville, Apr. 11, 1765: Murray—Grenville Papers, Whately file. The letter could, of course, be misdated—but not by much. Whately referred to the question of securities for distributors, a question put by Brettell to Jenkinson on Mar. 26.

ment to the contrary,[3] that the Grenville administration had sincerely meant to allow the colonies an alternative to a stamp act. The government not only intended to allow an alternative, but believed the colonies would present an acceptable one. The failure of North America to present a suitable scheme dismayed the ministry. Grenville had promised a stamp bill—and with his stubborn nature had shoved one through—but neither he nor his staff had prepared themselves sufficiently. They had depended utterly on American initiative, and when America failed them they had to jerry-build an administrative machine for their Stamp Act.

Several incidents, however, present a case equally strong against this interpretation. Both McCulloh and Mr. X had been working steadily on a stamp bill a year before Grenville even offered the colonies their grace. Furthermore, on September 22, 1763, the treasury ordered the stamp commissioners "to prepare the draught of a bill to be presented to Parlt. for extending the stamp duties to the colonies."[4] Presumably the commissioners complied with the treasury order. As has been shown, all during 1764 work progressed on the American stamp act. Whately told Jenkinson on July 31, 1764: "I have wrote you a long letter about the stamp act which I hoped to have sent you by a messenger to-

[3] Edmund S. Morgan, "The Postponement of the Stamp Act," *William and Mary Quarterly*, 3d ser., VII (1950), 353-392, treats, with heavy documentation, the interim period between Grenville's proposal of a stamp bill and that bill's enactment into law. Morgan argues forcefully that Grenville's proposal to the colonial agents—that the colonies might be allowed to propound a different plan—was a shallow gesture and that the first lord had no intention of listening to anything the colonies would propose.

[4] P.R.O., T. 29/35, p. 165, minute of Sept. 22, 1763.

morrow."[5] Whately might have meant an English stamp act, but presumably he meant an American measure, since he had written to Temple a month earlier of a colonial stamp act. Other expert advice was sought from the customs and the board of trade in 1764. Confusion—or mystery—still enshrouds much of the Stamp Act.

Perhaps only two features, from an administrative point of view, remain clear. First, Grenville apparently had little to do either with the proposing, working out the details, or planning the administration of the Stamp Act. Such tasks went to an array of subministers, chief of whom was Thomas Whately. His plan, with some reservations, and despite some defects, formed the basic foundation for the Stamp Act. Whately, of course, called upon the talents of McCulloh, Mr. X, John Pownall, the stamp commissioners, John Temple, Jared Ingersoll, and various colonial governors. Grenville, as the responsible minister, approved the work and saw to its passage through Parliament. The second clear feature seems to be that the Stamp Act, for all its reverberations in America, was poorly conceived, poorly planned, and over-hastily passed, despite the glitter of talent that went into its construction—probably the most extensive and diversified array of subministerial expertise that ever contributed to an American measure. Indeed, it seems to represent, as much as the many measures of the nineteenth century, that "fit of absent-mindedness" characteristic of the British Empire far more than it represents the evil designs of wicked ministers.

[5] Thomas Whately to Charles Jenkinson, July 31, 1764: B.M., MSS Add. 38,197, ff. 259-260.

SELECT BIBLIOGRAPHY

UNPUBLISHED SOURCES

Public Record Office and British Museum

The in-letters to any of the public offices such as the admiralty reveal more of the work and ideas of secretaries and undersecretaries to departments other than the admiralty, since those letters came to the admiralty from other departments. The Admiralty 1 series, in-letters, prove fruitful. Adm. 1/3819-3820—letters to the admiralty secretary from colonial governors during the period 1759-1790—concern many aspects of colonial affairs, from descriptions of military operations to questions concerning vice-admiralty courts. Volume 3820 has several drafts of letters in the terrible handwriting of Philip Stephens. Adm. 1/3866—in-letters to the admiralty secretary from the secretary to the customs, from 1757 to 1780—usually request naval help to fight smuggling and deputations to naval officers to act as customs officials. Although unfoliated and not placed in correct chronological order, they aid greatly in determining customs-admiralty relations. Adm. 1/4125-4147, informal letters from the secretaries of state to the admiralty, show more clearly than formal communications the interchange of ideas between the two departments. One of the most interesting features of this series is a group of private letters from undersecretaries of state to the admiralty secretary. Letters from the treasury to the admiralty may be found in Adm. 1/4286-4288, which covers the period 1757 to 1782. The table of contents in each of these volumes aids the interested reader greatly. The letters, generally official, often include inclosures of customs letters to the treasury. Most of the letters are addressed to the admiralty secretary from the treasury secretary and concern such matters as requests for navy estimates, requests for lists of ships, and information on convoys. Adm. 1/4327-4329, letters from the war office to the admiralty secretary, concern transportation, deserters, prisoners of war, and other matters.

Common out-letters from the admiralty during the period 1760-1782 are found in Adm. 2/715-750. These out-letters, bound in huge volumes, represent the secretary's correspondence on all sorts of matters relating to the navy—leaves, reprisals, appointment of subordinate officers, and so on. The letters are, however, formal and by their nature cannot show the extent of secretarial initiative in naval matters. Adm. 2/531-575, admiralty out-letters to admirals and public offices from 1760 to 1782, are found in huge, heavy, and unwieldy volumes. The correspondence concerns naval matters all over the world, from Cartagena to Calcutta. Usually the letters deal with such details as convoys, orders to admirals, and dispatches. The letters, also formal, are of value mainly as a check against other sources. Adm. 2/1057 concerns vice-admiralty business in England and America from 1762 to 1776. The many letters to the admiralty solicitor show his various duties and give some insight into the working of the vice-admiralty courts.

The Admiralty 3 series is the most important source for determining the structure of the admiralty. Only a thorough reading of Adm. 3/36-94, admiralty minutes from 1727 through 1782, provides an understanding of the hiring and firing policies of the admiralty, salaries, duties, and numbers of clerks, duties of the secretary, and all other business relating to the internal functioning of the admiralty.

Sources for both the treasury and the customs are found in the treasury papers, since the treasury held jurisdiction over, and worked in close cooperation with, the customs. The Treasury 1 series, especially volumes 430 to 531, proved a most valuable source. This loosely filed series of in-letters represents correspondence with the treasury from other departments, some of it formal, but much of it informal. The series contains many proposals to the treasury from various offices and persons regarding American measures. T. 29/35-51, treasury minutes from 1762 to 1782, reveal the structure of the treasury and provide a check on treasury reaction to proposals submitted to it. T. 11/26-28, out-letters to the customs and excise from 1759 to 1769, help assess customs-treasury relations and ascertain how often the treasury and customs secretaries corresponded independently of official authorization, indicating how much "leeway" they had. T. 27/28-34, general treasury out-letters from 1759 to 1783, and T. 28/1-2, out-letters to America, are of some use. T. 43/5-7 list the customs quarterly establishment from 1767 to 1774, an aid to the understanding of customs structure.

Select Bibliography

The work of the undersecretaries of state and the structure of the state departments may be studied in the state papers. Unfortunately, some of the material in this series is not so helpful as could be expected. S.P. 44/148-149, for instance, is disappointing, since the series consists of official letters, which, aside from illustrating the numerous matters with which the undersecretary dealt, contains little of interest. Yet this series includes the letter books of undersecretaries of state from 1724 to 1771. S.P. 44/138-143, letter books of the secretaries of state from 1760 to 1782, have many entries by undersecretaries. The various fees accruing to the secretary of state's office are listed in S.P. 45-30-35, which covers the period 1761-1782. Many of the important state papers are outlined in the *Calendar of Home Office Papers*, 1760 to 1775. Important papers covering the period after 1775, especially 1777 to 1782, are found in S.P. 37/12-15. These letters, correspondence between the undersecretaries, customs secretaries, and treasury secretaries, concern spies, smuggling, and a host of other matters relating to internal affairs during the war, as well as comments upon the course of the war on the battlefields of America and the diplomatic fields of Europe. Many of the letters are private and informal. These letters supplement, and in many cases duplicate, the correspondence in the C.O. 5 series, available on microfilm at the Library of Congress.

Several collections of papers in the British Museum are as important as documents in the Public Record Office. Perhaps the most valuable are the Liverpool papers, MSS Add. 38,197-38,470. Although Ninetta Jucker has published some of the Jenkinson papers for the years 1760 to 1766, she has omitted many important letters. Nearly every minor man of importance, and all of those discussed who were contemporaries of Jenkinson, corresponded with Jenkinson. The Hardwicke papers, MSS Add. 35,353-35,637 and 35,910-35,916, yield valuable information on the work of some of the secretaries and disclose important material relating to American policy. MSS Add. 41,355, the miscellaneous papers of Samuel Martin, Jr., secretary to the treasury, and MSS Add. 41,347-41,348, correspondence between Secretary Martin and his father, although skimpy, give some insight into the relations of a treasury secretary to his department. The Phelps papers, MSS Stowe 257-

259, show the undersecretary's many tasks and illustrate the relations between an undersecretary and his superior. The Newcastle papers, MSS Add. 32,679-33,201, are invaluable. Much important information on minor men, biographical and otherwise, through the year 1765 can be gleaned from the voluminous Newcastle manuscripts.

William L. Clements Library

The Shelburne papers are a most valuable collection at the Clements Library. The extensive papers dealing with colonial affairs are useful, and the Shelburne papers are nearly the only source for biographical material on Maurice Morgann. The Knox papers, although useful and complete, contain little of importance not already calendared by the Historical Manuscripts Commission. Other manuscripts of some value included the Germain, Clinton, Dowdeswell, and Sidney papers.

Other Sources

The Dartmouth papers at the William Salt Library, Stafford, reveal Pownall's influence at the American department more clearly than any other source. The Historical Manuscripts Commission calendared the Dartmouth papers so poorly that not only are letters of importance omitted in the Commission's report, but others are described so briefly as to give a completely wrong impression of their contents. Information on Pownall's family, lands, titles, deeds, and other personal matters can be gathered from the Pownall papers at the Lincoln Record Office. The Monson papers at the Lincoln Record Office were also of some help. Sir John Murray's collection of Grenville papers in London has some important letters of Thomas Whately not published in the four volume edition of the *Grenville Papers*. The Sandwich papers, at Mapperton Manor in Dorset, show the relationships between Sandwich and Secretary Stephens, although the most important exchanges between the two have been published in the four volume edition of *Sandwich Papers*. The correspondence of Undersecretary Edward Weston at Farmington, Connecticut, like the Knox papers, has been well calendared by the Historical Manuscripts Commission. The wills of the minor men, sometimes important for biographical information, are located at Somerset House, the Strand, London.

PUBLISHED SOURCES

Several publications of the Historical Manuscripts Commission are the best source for studying the private life, the public work, and the influence of the subministers. The Knox manuscripts, *Report on Manuscripts in Various Collections*, vi (Dublin, 1906), cover every aspect of Knox's public and private life. This report and the Weston papers, *Reports on the Manuscripts of the Earl of Eglinton, Sir J. Stirling Maxwell, Bart., C. S. H. Drummond Moray, Esq., C. F. Weston-Underwood, Esq., and G. Wingfield Digby, Esq.* (London, 1885), are two of the most valuable sets of published papers relating to eighteenth-century minor men. Although Weston held office during a period earlier than that covered by this work, his papers nonetheless provide valuable information on the life and labor of a permanent undersecretary of state. The *Tenth Report, Appendix, Part VI* (London, 1885), contains some of the letters of John Robinson. Especially interesting is his correspondence with Charles Jenkinson concerning the general election of 1784. The *Report on the Manuscripts of the Earl of Dartmouth*, i (London, 1887), ii (London, 1895), and *The Manuscripts of Mrs. Stopford-Sackville at Drayton House, Northamptonshire*, i (London, 1904), ii (London, 1910), are indispensable for studying the relations between undersecretaries of state and their superiors. The *American Manuscripts in the Royal Institution of Great Britain*, ii (Dublin, 1906), iii (Hereford, 1907), iv (Hereford, 1909), show Morgann at his best, helping General Carleton in New York to help the Loyalists. The papers of Lord Carlisle, *Fifteenth Report, Part IX* (London, 1895), contain several letters of Undersecretary William Eden, sent over with Carlisle as a peace commissioner.

The publications of the Historical Manuscripts Commission are the best source for studying both the public and private lives of minor men, but various collections of state papers and parliamentary documents often give better insights into their official work and the offices with which they were connected. The *Reports of the Commissioners Appointed by Act 25 Geo.*

III. cap. 19 to Enquire into the Fees, Gratuities, Perquisites and Emoluments, which are or have been lately Received in Several Public Offices therein Mentioned (London, 1806) is indispensable for anyone wishing to examine the structure of the admiralty and the office of secretary of state, and the place of secretaries and undersecretaries in that structure. The *Fourteenth Report of the Commissioners Appointed to Examine, Take, and State the Public accounts of the Kingdom* (London, 1786) describes in detail the English customs system. For the board of trade and John Pownall's place in it, see the *Journal of the Commissioners for Trade and Plantations, 1734/5-1741* (London, 1930) through 1776-1782 (London, 1938). The *Calendar of Treasury Papers, 1697-1701/2* (London, 1871) through 1742-1745 (London, 1903), unfortunately has not been completed beyond the dates indicated. It nonetheless furnishes many examples of the official interchanges between the treasury and customs secretaries. Official correspondence among all the subministers on matters domestic, colonial, and foreign is outlined in Joseph Reddington and Richard Arthur Roberts, eds., *Calendar of Home Office Papers of the Reign of George III* (4 vols., London, 1878-1899). The volumes cover the period 1760 to 1775.

Speaking on departmental business in Parliament was an important part of the work of some of the minor men, especially the treasury secretaries. The two most useful collections of parliamentary debates for this study are William Cobbett, ed., *The Parliamentary History of England from the Earliest Period to the Year 1803,* xv (London, 1813) through xxiii (London, 1814), which cover the years 1753 to 1783, and John Almon, ed., *The Parliamentary Register: or, History of the Proceedings and Debates of the House of Commons [House of Lords],* 1774-1780 (17 vols., London, 1775-1780). This series is continued by John Debrett with the same title to the year 1796 in 45 volumes. Almon, more complete than Cobbett, was used for debates after 1774. The fate of any legislation, proposed by minor men and others, may be followed in *Journals of the House of Commons,* 1757 to 1784, vols. xxix–xxxviii, and *Journals of the House of Lords,* 1756 to 1787, vols. xxix–xxxviii.

Official correspondence between subministers and colonial

Pa., 1930-1933); and J. E. Norton, ed., *The Letters of Edward Gibbon* (2 vols., London, 1956), II. The most important sources for the correspondence of Pownall's colleague William Knox include: Lila M. Hawes, "Letters to the Georgia Colonial Agent, July 1762 to January 1771," *Georgia Historical Quarterly*, XXXVI (1952); "Garth Correspondence," scattered throughout vols. XXVI (1926) through XXXIII (1932) of the *South Carolina Historical and Genealogical Magazine*; and *The Letters of Hon. James Habersham, 1756-1775* (Collections of the Georgia Historical Society, VI [Atlanta, 1904]). Undersecretary Morgann's work in Quebec is commented upon in William S. Wallace, ed., *The Maseres Letters, 1766-1768* (University of Toronto Studies, History and Economics, III, 2 [Toronto, 1919]). Several of Whately's letters are published in William James Smith, ed., *The Grenville Papers: Being the Correspondence of Richard Grenville, Earl Temple, K.G., and the Right Hon. George Grenville, their Friends and Contemporaries* (4 vols., London, 1852-1853); *Ingersoll Papers* (New Haven Colony Historical Society Collections, IX [New Haven, 1918]); and *Correspondence of John Russell, Fourth Duke of Bedford*, Introduction by Lord John Russell (3 vols., London, 1846). There are several interesting letters of Whately's colleague Grey Cooper in *The Private Correspondence of David Garrick with the most Celebrated Persons of his Time: Now First Published from the Originals, and Illustrated with Notes, and a New Biographical Memoir of Garrick* (2 vols., London, 1831-1832). Correspondence of, and references to, Philip Stephens are found in G. R. Barnes and J. H. Owen, eds., *The Private Papers of John, Earl of Sandwich* (Publications of the Navy Records Society, LIX [1923], LXXI [1933], LXXV [1936], and LXXVIII [1938]); and Sir John Knox Laughton, ed., *The Letters and Papers of Charles, Lord Barham, Admiral of the Red Squadron, 1758-1813* (Publications of the Navy Records Society, XXXII [1907], XXXVIII [1910], and XXXIX [1911]). The civil-servant opinions expressed by Admiralty Secretary Corbett are found in Brian Tunstall, ed., *The Byng Papers, Selected from the Letters and Papers of Admiral Sir George Byng, First Viscount Torrington, and of his Son, Admiral the Hon. John Byng* (3 vols., Publications of the Navy Records Society, LXVII

[1930], LXVIII [1931], LXX [1932]), III. Of lesser importance, but valuable for showing one admiral's hostile attitude toward the admiralty, is D. Bonner-Smith, ed., *The Barrington Papers, Selected from the Letters and Papers of Admiral the Hon. Samuel Barrington* (Publications of the Navy Records Society, LXXVII [1937], LXXXI [1941]).

Two series of correspondence includes letters of, and reference to, several of the secretaries and undersecretaries. They are: Sir John Fortescue, ed., *The Correspondence of King George the Third* (6 vols., London, 1927-1928), vol. I of which must be checked for errors in Sir Lewis Namier, *Additions and Corrections to Sir John Fortescue's Edition of the Correspondence of King George the Third* (Manchester, 1937); and Benjamin Franklin Stevens, *Facsimiles of Manuscripts in European Archives Relating to America* (London, 1889-1895).

Other correspondence consulted, both for reference to the subministers and a general picture of the important figures and their ideas during the period, includes Romney Sedgwick, ed., *Letters from George III to Lord Bute, 1756-1766* (London, 1939); Philip C. Yorke, *The Life and Correspondence of Philip Yorke, Earl of Hardwicke, Lord High Chancellor of Great Britain* (3 vols., Cambridge, 1913); George Thomas Albemarle, *Memoirs of the Marquis of Rockingham and his Contemporaries* (2 vols., London, 1852); Lord Edmond Fitzmaurice, *Life of William, Earl of Shelburne* (3 vols., London, 1875-1876); Rev. Thomas Keppel, *The Life of Augustus Keppel, Admiral of the White, and First Lord of the Admiralty* (2 vols., London, 1842); and Sir John Barrow, *The Life of George, Lord Anson* (London, 1839). The works on Hardwicke, Rockingham, Shelburne, Keppel, and Anson are biographies. They are included under the heading of correspondence because their value lay not in the writing of the biographers, but in the many letters, published in full, to and from the subjects of the biographies.

The pamphlets written by the minor men—pamphlets on politics and other subjects—were as important as any other source in giving the ideas, political and otherwise, of the subministers. Knox was a prolific writer, and much was gleaned from a study of his publications. His *Extra Official State Papers*,

Addressed to the Right Hon. Lord Rawdon and the other Members of the two Houses of Parliament Associated for the Preservation of the Constitution and Promoting the Prosperity of the British Empire (Dublin, 1789) show the undersecretary's important participation in the first measures designed to free Irish trade and Knox's own estimate of his importance to government. Knox's pamphlet, *Helps to a Right Decision upon the Merits of the Late Treaty of Commerce with France, Addressed to the Members of both Houses of Parliament* (London, 1787), reveals the extent of the former agent's bitterness toward America: he was enthusiastic over the proposed freer trade with France just four years after he had tried to squash free trade between America and the British West Indies. Knox wrote several political broadsides, many of which are discussed in the text. These pamphlets are: *A Letter to a Member of Parliament wherein the Power of the British Legislature and the Case of the Colonists are Briefly and Impartially Considered* (London, 1765); *An Appendix to the Present State of the Nation, Containing a Reply to Observations on that Pamphlet* (London, 1769); *The Claim of the Colonies to an Exemption from Internal Taxes Imposed by Authority of Parliament Examined* (London, 1765); *The Controversy between Great Britain and her Colonies Reviewed; the Several Pleas of the Colonies in Support of their Right to all the Liberties and Privileges of British Subjects, and to Exemption from the Legislative Authority of Parliament, Stated and Considered; and the Nature of their Connection with, and Dependence on, Great Britain, Shown upon the Evidence of Historical Facts and Authentic Records* (London, 1769); *The Interest of the Merchants and Manufacturers of Great Britain in the Present Contest with the Colonies Stated and Considered* (London, 1774); *The Justice and Policy of the Late Act of Parliament for Making more Effectual Provision for the Government of the Province of Quebec, Asserted and Proved; and the Conduct of Administration Respecting that Province Stated and Vindicated* (London, 1774); and *The Present State of the Nation Particularly with Respect to its Trade, Finances, &c.&c., Addressed to the King and both Houses of Parliament* (London, 1768).

Select Bibliography

Whately was a prolific writer of political tracts, as well as the author of a widely acclaimed essay on gardening. He was also a student of Shakespeare. Whately showed the last two interests in his *Observations on Modern Gardening, Illustrated by Descriptions* (London, 1770) and *Remarks on some of the Characters of Shakespeare* (London, 1785). His political tracts include: *Considerations on the Trade and Finances of this Kingdom, and on the Measures of Administration, with Respect to those Great National Objects since the Conclusion of the Peace*, in *A Collection of Scarce and interesting Tracts* (2 vols., London, 1787-1788), II; *The Regulations lately made Concerning the Colonies and the Taxes Imposed upon them Considered* (London, 1765); and *Remarks on the Budget*, in *A Collection of Scarce and Interesting Tracts*, I. Whately's successor, Grey Cooper, used his talent with the political pen to gain office, an event that makes Cooper's works, *A Pair of Spectacles for Short Sighted Politicians: or, A Candid Answer to a Late Extraordinary Pamphlet, Entitled, An Honest Man's Reasons for Declining to take any Part in the New Administration* (London, 1765) and *The Merits of the New Administration Truly Stated; in Answer to the Several Pamphlets and Papers Published against Them* (London, 1765), especially interesting.

Other pamphlets which proved useful, some of them written by minor men, were: Edmund Burke, *Observations on a Late State of the Nation* (London, 1769), and *Thoughts on the Causes of the Present Discontents*, in Edward John Payne, ed., *Burke Select Works* (Oxford, 1887), I; Charles Carkesse, *The Act of Tonnage and Poundage and Rates of Merchandize, with the Further Subsidy: the 1/3 and 2/3 Subsidies: the Old Impost: the Additional Impost: and all other Duties Relating to His Majesties Customs, Payable upon any Sort of Merchandize Imported or Exported . . . to Which is Added by Way of Appendix, the Several Acts Which Passed the Last Session to the Customs, with the Additional Book of Rates of Goods and Merchandize Usually Imported . . . Together with an Alphabetical Index to the Whole* (London, 1726); David Hartley, *The Budget, Inscribed to the Man, who thinks Himself Minister*, in *A Collection of Scarce and Interesting Tracts*, I; Charles

Select Bibliography

Lloyd, *An Honest Man's Reasons for Declining to Take Part in the New Administration* (London, 1765), in *A Collection of Scarce and Interesting Tracts*, II, and *The Conduct of the Late Administration Examined, with an Appendix Containing Original and Authentic Documents* (London, 1767); John Locke, *Further Considerations Concerning Raising the Value of Money Wherein Mr. Lowndes's Arguments for it in his Late Report Concerning an Essay for the Amendment of Silver Coins, are Particularly Considered* (London, 1695); William Lowndes, *A Report Containing an Essay for the Amendment of Silver Coins* (London, 1695); and Thomas Pownall, *The Administration of the Colonies, Wherein their Rights and Constitution are Discussed and Stated* (London, 1768).

The articles which subministers contributed to contemporary periodicals, while not revealing their characters in so much detail as do the pamphlets, are nonetheless helpful. The following articles are useful: John Pownall, *"Letter to the Rev. James Douglas, F.A.S., from John Pownall, Esq., on a Roman Tile found at Reculver in Kent," Archaeologia: or Miscellaneous Tracts Relating to Antiquity*, VIII (1787); John Pownall, *"Account of Some Sepulchral Antiquities Discovered at Lincoln," Archaeologia*, X (1792); and Thomas Pownall, *"Memoire on the Roman Earthen Ware Fished up Within the Mouth of the River Thames," Archaeologia*, V (1779).

A few diaries and memoirs provide the "feel" of the eighteenth century, especially the period under discussion. Cecil Aspinall-Oglander, *Admiral's Wife, The Life and Letters of Mrs. Edward Boscawen, 1719-1761* (London, 1940), has many extracts from Mrs. Boscawen's journal, valuable for their references to Cleveland. Richard Cumberland, *Memoirs Written by Himself Containing an Account of his Life and Writings, Interspersed with Anecdotes and Characters of Several of the Most Distinguished Persons of his Time, with Whom he had had Intercourse and Connexion* (2 vols., London, 1807), shows the remarkable versatility of the board of trade secretary who replaced Pownall and notes some of the inner workings of the board of trade. P. O. Hutchinson, ed., *The Diary and Letters of His Excellency Thomas Hutchinson, Esq.* (2 vols., London, 1883-1886), I, occasionally mentions John Pownall. John

Select Bibliography

Nichols, *Literary Anecdotes of the Eighteenth Century* . . . (9 vols., London, 1812-1815), VI, lists the outside interests of Treasury Secretary West. Sir Nathaniel William Wraxall, *Historical and Posthumous Memoirs*, introduced by Richard Askham (London, 1904), comments upon the parliamentary relationship between Cooper and North. For a gossipy picture of the age in which minor men lived, Horace Walpole's *Memoirs of the Reign of George III* (4 vols., London, 1894), inaccurate and biased as it is, yet remains the most interesting.

Some compilations of source documents dealing with events, men, and offices are useful as time-savers, for they often publish sources which can be found elsewhere only by spending an excessive amount of time going through other records. J. C. Beaglehole, ed., *The Journals of Captain James Cook on his Voyages of Discovery* (Cambridge, Eng., 1955), pp. 605-622, lists all the official correspondence between the various subordinate departments of the admiralty relative to the outfitting of the *Endeavour*. One key to understanding the admiralty is to see how swiftly it could outfit a ship for service and how it accomplished this task. Beaglehole provides such information. Arthur L. Cross, *Eighteenth-Century Documents Relating to the Royal Forests, the Sheriffs, and Smuggling* (New York, 1938), has many papers relating to the customs board. *Franklin Before the Privy Council* (Boston, 1855), gives an account of Franklin's ordeal and reprints the letters of Hutchinson, Oliver, and Whately that led to it. Vincent Harlow and Frederick Madden, *British Colonial Developments, 1774-1834* (Oxford, 1948), has an account of Knox defending his attitude toward American-West Indian trade after the Revolution, a good account of Knox's motivation in drafting the order-in-council of 1783. Adam Shortt and Arthur G. Doughty, eds., *Documents Relating to the Constitutional History of Canada* (2 vols., Ottawa, 1907), I, prints many of the documents relevant to the Proclamation of 1763 and the Quebec Act. Samuel Eliot Morison, ed., *Sources and Documents Illustrating the American Revolution, 1764-1788, and the Formation of the Federal Constitution* (Oxford, 1948), is a useful reference for American reaction to British colonial legislation.

Several contemporary journals, periodicals, anecdotal pam-

phlets, and books contain useful biographical information—
dates of birth and death, offices held by minor men in any
year, salaries of various public offices, important events, and
so on. Though this material is sometimes inaccurate, it often
gives important data. The most valuable of these sources are:
John Almon, *Biographical, Literary, and Political Ancedotes
of Several of the Most Eminent Persons of the Present Age* (3
vols., London, 1797); Robert Beatson, *A Political Index to the
Histories of Great Britain and Ireland: or A Complete Register
of the Hereditary Honours, Public Offices, and Persons in
Office from the Earliest Periods to the Present Time* (3 vols.,
London, 1806); *The Annual Register*, III (London, 1760)
through XXVI (London, 1785); *The Gentleman's Magazine*, XXX
(London, 1760) through LXXX (London, 1810); and *The Court
and City Register*. This last journal was published in London
annually, and the volumes from 1750 to 1783 are of use.

SECONDARY WORKS

Works dealing with the history of the civil service are generally unsatisfactory. Many authors tend to oversimplify conditions in the eighteenth century, making the entire service
appear inefficient and corrupt, so that the reforms of the
nineteenth century shine like beacon lights on a rocky coast.
These authors contended that nineteenth-century reforms
"made" the service, and they bring out only the worst aspects
of the eighteenth century in order to prove it. Herman Finer,
The British Civil Service (London, 1937), and Robert Moses,
The Civil Service of Great Britain (New York, 1914), while
biased, are more reliable in scholarship than most. Of some
help were Sir John Craig, *A History of Red Tape, An Account
of the Origin and Development of the Civil Service* (London,
1955), and S. E. Finer, "Patronage and the Public Service,"
Public Administration, XXX (1952), 329-360.

Works that specialize in the history and structure of one
governmental department are of far greater value than works
on the history of the civil service. The admiralty, unfortunately, has received no detailed study of its structure in the
eighteenth century. The only work that attempts to trace the
evolution of admiralty administration is the series of articles

Select Bibliography

by Sir Oswyn A. R. Murray, "The Admiralty," *Mariner's Mirror*, XXIII (1937), 13-35, 129-147, 316-331; XXIV (1938), 101-104, 204-225, 330-352, 458-478; XXV (1939), 89-111, 216-228, 328-338. G. F. James, "Josiah Burchett, Secretary to the Lords Commissioners of the Admiralty," *Mariner's Mirror*, XXIII (1937), 477-498, shows the place of the first permanent admiralty secretary in the admiralty structure. William Laird Clowes, *The Royal Navy, A History from the Earliest Times to the Present* (4 vols., Boston, 1897-1899), devotes some space to admiralty administration. The classic study by Robert G. Albion, *Forests and Sea Power: the Timber Problem of the Royal Navy, 1652-1862* (Harvard Economic Studies, XXXIX [Cambridge, Mass., 1926]), presents in some detail the administration of Lord Sandwich during the American Revolution. Joseph C. Doty, *The British Admiralty Board as a Factor in Colonial Administration, 1689-1763* (Philadelphia, 1930), has some useful information, although the work is sketchy and sometimes inaccurate. Carl Ubbelohde, *The Vice-Admiralty Courts and the American Revolution* (Chapel Hill, 1960), describes well the vice-admiralty court at Halifax.

Several studies of the board of trade have been published that, when examined in conjunction with one another, give a complete and detailed picture of the organization. Charles M. Andrews, *The Colonial Period of American History* (4 vols., New Haven, 1934-1938), IV, presents an accurate general account of the board of trade (as well as of vice-admiralty courts). Oliver M. Dickerson, *American Colonial Government, 1695-1765* (Cleveland, 1912), although less accurate than Andrews, studies the board in more detail. Dickerson should be checked against Arthur H. Basye, *The Lords Commissioners of Trade and Plantations, 1748-1782* (New Haven, 1925). Mary P. Clarke, "The Board of Trade at Work," *American Historical Review*, XVII (1912), 17-43, has a detailed description of the secretary's work.

The treasury, the financial center of eighteenth-century administration, has been examined at length by J. E. D. Binney, *British Public Administration and Finance, 1774-1792* (Oxford, 1958), an indispensable work. Edward Hughes, *Studies in Administration and Finance* (Manchester, 1934), is helpful. Dora Mae Clark, *The Rise of the British Treasury* (New Haven, 1960), summarizes the treasury's role in politics and policy. A necessary guide for anyone studying minor men at the treasury is Clark, "The Office of Secretary to the Treasury in the Eighteenth Century," *American Historical Review,* XLII (1936-1937), 22-45. William T. Laprade, "Public Opinion and the General Election of 1784," *English Historical Review,* XXXI (1916), 224-237, shows the work of a former treasury secretary in a general election.

Mark A. Thomson, *The Secretaries of State, 1681-1782* (Oxford, 1932), is an excellent introduction to the various state departments. A necessary book for anyone wishing to study the American department is Margaret M. Spector, *The American Department of the British Government* (Columbia Univ. Studies in History, Economics, and Public Law, 466 [New York, 1940]). Spector outlines the working of the American department thoroughly and clarifies the relation between the American department and the older secretariats. The amount of patronage it could control measured in part a department's influence, and B. D. Bargar, "Lord Dartmouth's Patronage, 1772-1775," *William and Mary Quarterly,* 3d ser., XV (1958), 191-200, shows how the American department under Dartmouth gained control of nearly all colonial patronage. G. H. Guttridge, "Lord George Germain in Office," *American Historical Review,* XXXIII (1928), 23-43, considers the American department incompetently managed by Germain during the Revolution. Alan Valentine, in his more recent *Lord George Germain* (Oxford, 1962), seconds the judgment, although he perhaps credits Germain with more intelligence than did Guttridge. Gerald Saxon Brown, however, in his *The American Secretary, The Colonial Policy of Lord George Germain, 1775-1778* (Ann Arbor, 1963), argues convincingly that Germain was not only competent, but usually right in his strategic judgments. The incompetence of generals in the field and the overruling of the secretary's opinions by the cabinet accounted for the disaster to British arms at Saratoga and the escape of the French fleet from the Mediterranean. D. B. Horn, *The British Diplomatic Service, 1689-1789* (Oxford, 1961), focuses, as its title indicates, on the administration of diplomacy. Yet it also touches on the organization of the state departments.

Perhaps the best administrative study of any government department in the eighteenth century is Elizabeth E. Hoon, *The Organization of the English Customs System, 1696-1786* (New York, 1938). Hoon's work is detailed, accurate, and readable. Other works on various aspects of the customs include Dixon G. Graham, "Notes on the Records of the Custom House, London," *English Historical Review*, XXXIV (1919), 71-84, and B. R. Leftwich, "The Later History and Administration of the Custom Revenue in England," *Transactions of the Royal Historical Society*, 4th ser., XIII (1930), 187-203. W. R. Ward, "Some Eighteenth-Century Civil Servants: the English Revenue Commissioners, 1754-98," *English Historical Review*, LXX (1955), gives the background and political connections of the customs commissioners.

An assessment of secretarial influence on British actions before and during the American Revolution necessitates a clear understanding of the major events—political decisions, parliamentary acts, ministerial changes, colonial actions, military operations, and so on—between 1763 and 1783. For a general picture of these major events, see Lawrence Henry Gipson, *The Coming of the Revolution, 1763-1775* (New York, 1954); John R. Alden, *The American Revolution, 1775-1783* (New York, 1954); Charles R. Ritcheson, *British Politics and the American Revolution* (Norman, Okla., 1954); Eric Robson, *The American Revolution in its Political and Military Aspects, 1763-1783* (New York, 1955); John C. Miller, *Origins of the American Revolution* (Boston, 1943); and the administrative study of the logistical problems of the British army during the Revolution, Edward E. Curtis, *The Organization of the British Army in the American Revolution* (Yale Historical Publications, Miscellany, XIX [New Haven, 1926]). Piers Mackesy, *The War for America, 1775-1783* (Cambridge, Mass., 1964), offers the newest and most thorough assessment of the war from the vantage point of Whitehall. Of some help are G. S. Graham, *British Policy and Canada, 1774-1791* (New York, 1930); R. A. Humphreys, "British Colonial Policy and the American Revolution," *History*, XIX (1935), 42-48; and Charles R. Ritcheson, "The American Revolution: Its Influence on the Development

Select Bibliography

of the British Empire," *Parliamentary Affairs, the Journal of the Hansard Society,* IV (1951), 245-260.

The first work to examine at length British political maneuvering during the earlier years of George III's reign and relate such politicking to American colonial policy was Clarence W. Alvord, *The Mississippi Valley in British Politics* (2 vols., Cleveland, 1917). Alvord is of some use, although Humphreys has proved him wrong in many of his interpretations of colonial policy, and Jack M. Sosin, *Whitehall and the Wilderness* (Lincoln, Neb., 1961), revises and nearly supersedes Alvord. The works of the Namier school have also found errors in Alvord. They study the politics and politicians of the period 1763-1783, but fail, except in rare instances, to relate the politics and politicians to colonial policy. Sir Lewis Namier and John Brooke, *Charles Townshend* (New York, 1964), for example, although it admits that only Townshend's influence on American policy justifies a study of his life, devotes the overwhelming majority of its pages to matters other than those relating to America. Such studies are nonetheless necessary for anyone wishing to grasp in detail the factional maneuvering and the motivations of major political figures. The more important works include: Sir Lewis B. Namier, *England in the Age of the American Revolution* (London, 1930, 2d ed., 1961), *The Structure of Politics at the Accession of George III* (London, 1957), and *Crossroads of Power* (New York, 1962); John Brooke, *The Chatham Administration, 1766-1768* (London, 1956); Ian R. Christie, *The End of North's Ministry, 1780-1782* (London, 1958); and Richard Pares, *King George III and the Politicians* (Oxford, 1953). Pares is so outstanding in his own right that it is perhaps unfair to consider him of the Namier school, although he has accepted basically Namier's interpretation of the political structure of the period. Herbert Butterfield, *George III and the Historians* (London, 1957), attempts to refute some of the Namierite interpretations, but falls into several errors himself.

Many of the British acts that led to the American Revolution, and the ministers who took responsibility for them, have been studied in detail. R. A. Humphreys, "Lord Shelburne and the Proclamation of 1763," *English Historical Review,*

XLIX (1934), 241-264, discusses the proclamation and the events that led to it. American reaction to the Stamp Act is thoroughly treated by Edmund S. and Helen M. Morgan, *The Stamp Act Crisis* (Chapel Hill, 1953), while Edmund S. Morgan, "The Postponement of the Stamp Act," *William and Mary Quarterly*, 3d ser., VII (1950), 353-392, analyzes the motives of George Grenville in passing the measure. Charles R. Ritcheson, "The Preparation of the Stamp Act," *William and Mary Quarterly*, 3d ser., X (1953), 543-559, attempts to discover the author of the Stamp Act. Although Ritcheson identifies the wrong man as the author, he nonetheless provides some valuable material relating to the origins of the measure. Jack P. Greene, " 'A Dress of Horror!' Henry McCulloh's Objections to the Stamp Act," *Huntington Library Quarterly*, XXVI (1963), 253-262, for the first time presents the written statement of opposition to the act by the man long considered its creator. F. J. Ericson, "The Contemporary British Opposition to the Stamp Act," *Michigan Academy of Science, Arts, and Letters*, XXIX (1944), 489-505, asserts that British opposition to the proposed stamp bill forced Grenville to postpone passage of the measure. The Sugar Act, a part of Grenville's revenue-raising schemes that provoked a less violent reaction than the Stamp Act, is studied by Allen S. Johnson, "The Passage of the Sugar Act," *William and Mary Quarterly*, 3d ser., XVI (1959), 507-514. The Townshend duties and their American consequences are assessed by Oliver M. Dickerson, *The Navigation Acts and the American Revolution* (Philadelphia, 1951), and "England's most Fateful Decision," *New England Quarterly*, XXII (1949), 388-394. Dora Mae Clark, "The American Board of Customs, 1767-1783," *American Historical Review*, XLV (1940), 777-806, discusses the relations between the American board, the British treasury, and colonial officials. Several historians have written on various aspects of the Quebec Act. Reginald Coupland, *The Quebec Act: A Study in Statesmanship* (Oxford, 1925), praises Carleton and Carleton's part in the measure, almost to the point of idolatry. R. A. Humphreys and S. Morley Scott, "Lord Northington and Laws of Canada," *Canadian Historical Review*, XIV (1933), 42-61, traces the earlier attempts to ameliorate the lot of the French Canadians. Louise P. Kellogg, "A Footnote to the Quebec Act," *Canadian Historical Review*, XIII (1932), 147-156, shows that the Quebec Act provided civil government for those people in the western territories, Illinois, Indiana, and Wisconsin, who had been without civil government since 1763 as a result of the proclamation of that year.

A few special works proved of particular interest regarding men, policy, and events not related to any one colonial measure. Ella Lonn, *The Colonial Agents of the Southern Colonies* (Chapel Hill, 1945), by showing the origin and function of the agencies, points out one aspect of British-colonial relations not often discussed in detail by historians and gives some information on Knox's work for Georgia. Arthur M. Schlesinger, *The Colonial Merchants and the American Revolution* (Columbia Univ. Studies in History, Economics, and Public Law, LXXVIII [New York, 1918]), studies American merchant reaction to British legislation. Lucy Stuart Sutherland, "Edmund Burke and the first Rockingham Ministry," *English Historical Review*, XLVII (1932), 46-72, discusses Burke and the growth of merchant pressure on the British government for a loosening of colonial policy and the opposition between West Indian and North American merchants. R. A. Humphreys, "Lord Shelburne and British Colonial Policy, 1766-8," *English Historical Review*, L (1935), 257-277, analyzes Shelburne's ideas on colonial westward expansion and on economic reform. Eric Robson, "Lord North," *History Today*, II, 532-538, studies the ineffectiveness of North and asserts that this ineffectiveness explained the close cooperation between George III and such men as Robinson and Jenkinson. Herbert Butterfield, *George III, Lord North, and the People, 1779-1780* (London, 1949), focuses on the popular agitation against the government in England and the volunteer associations in Ireland. Butterfield condemns the "behind the stairs" activity of such men as Robinson. One aspect of the political life during the period—the political press —is well covered by Robert R. Rea, *The English Press in Politics, 1760-1774* (Lincoln, Neb., 1963).

BIBLIOGRAPHICAL AND BIOGRAPHICAL AIDS

To anyone interested in eighteenth-century Britain the most important bibliographical aid is Stanley Pargellis and D. J.

Select Bibliography

Medley, *Bibliography of British History: the Eighteenth Century, 1714-1789* (Oxford, 1951). Equally important for the study of men and colonial policy are: Charles M. Andrews, *Guide to the Materials for American History to 1783, in the Public Record Office of Great Britain* (2 vols., Washington, 1912-1914); Charles M. Andrews and F. G. Davenport, *Guide to the Manuscript Materials for the History of the United States to 1783, in the British Museum, in Minor London Archives, and in the Libraries of Oxford and Cambridge* (Washington, 1908); W. E. Ewing, *Guide to the Manuscript Collections in the William L. Clements Library* (Ann Arbor, 1952); and Grace Gardner Griffin, *A Guide to Manuscripts Relating to American History in British Depositories, Reproduced for the Division of Manuscripts of the Library of Congress* (Washington, 1946).

The most important biographical aid is Leslie Stephen and Sidney Lee, eds., *Dictionary of National Biography* (63 vols., London, 1885-1900). A supplementary 3 volumes was added in 1901 and the *D.N.B.* was reprinted in 1908-1909 in 22 volumes. The *Bulletin of the Institute of Historical Research* periodically corrects mistakes in the *D.N.B.* and adds supplementary material. Much less detailed, although it includes more men of the eighteenth century than the *D.N.B.*, is Sir George J. Armytage, ed., *Obituary Prior to 1800 (as far as Relates to England, Scotland, and Ireland)*, compiled by Sir William Musgrave (6 vols., Publications of the Harleian Society, XLV-XLX [London, 1899-1901]). Musgrave records the journal that gives the obituary notice for nearly every figure that attained any prominence in the eighteenth century. For those who attended universities, biographical material may be found in Joseph Foster, *Alumni Oxonienses, 1716-1786* (4 vols., Oxford, 1891), and John and S. A. Venn, *Alumni Cantabrigiensis* (4 vols., Cambridge, 1922-1927). G. R. Russel Barker and Alan H. Stenning, *The Records of Old Westminster* (2 vols., London, 1928), gives information on those minor men who attended Westminster school. Since many of the subministers accumulated enough property to become landed gentry, L. G. Pine, ed., *Burke's Genealogical and Heraldic History of the Landed Gentry*, seventeenth edition (London, 1952), was of value. Gerrit P. Judd, *Members of*

Parliament, 1734-1832 (New Haven, 1955), contained useful information on those minor men elected to the House of Commons. Often biographical material of various sorts—anecdotes concerning minor men or references to them—can be found in *Notes and Queries for Readers and Writers, Collectors and Librarians*, a periodical first published in London in 1850 and continued to the present. Other biographical aids of value were: G. E. Cokayne, *Complete Baronetage* (5 vols., London, 1900-1906), v; *The Record of the Royal Society of London*, 4th ed. (London, 1940); J. Bruce Williamson, *The Middle Temple Bench Book*, 2d ed. (London, 1938); *Register of Admissions to the Honourable Society of the Middle Temple from the Fifteenth Century to the year 1944* (London, 1949), compiled by H. A. C. Sturgess; John G. Nichols, *The Herald and Genealogist*, (8 vols., London, 1863-1874), vi; and *The Genealogist's Magazine*, vi (1932-1934). Two biographies, E. Jane Whately, *Life and Correspondence of Richard Whately, D.D., Late Archbishop of Dublin* (2 vols., London, 1866), i, and John A. Schutz, *Thomas Pownall, British Defender of American Liberty: a Study of Anglo-American Relations in the Eighteenth Century* (Old Northwest Historical Series, v [Glendale, Calif., 1951]), contain important information—Whately's for the family history of Thomas Whately, and Schutz's for the family history of John Pownall.

Several English local histories have useful biographical information. Those of most value are: John Hutchins, *The History and Antiquities of the County of Dorset* (Westminster, 1861); Charles James Feret, *Fulham Old and New: Being an Exhaustive History of the Ancient Parish of Fulham* (3 vols., London, 1900); Rev. Cannon A. R. Maddison, ed., *Lincolnshire Pedigrees* (London, 1904), iii; *Lincolnshire Church Notes made by William John Monson, F.S.A., Afterwards Sixth Lord Monson of Burton, 1820-1840* (Publications of the Lincoln Record Society, xxi [Hereford, 1936]); *Lincolnshire Notes and Queries*, ix (1907), xi (1911), xix (1928); and the manuscript in the British Museum, *Athena Suffolcienses: or, a Catalogue of Suffolk Authors with some Account of their Lives, and Lists of their Writings, vol. 3, During the Nineteenth Century* (1847).

INDEX

Index

customs, commissioners of, 87, 88, 102, 106, 107, 111, 114, 115, 116, 117, 118, 121, 123, 124, 127, 128, 129, 130, 131, 132, 133, 134, 135, 136, 136n, 137, 138, 139, 152, 167, 168, 183; assertions of independence from treasury, 52-54; blunder in allowing copper to reach France, 167; civil service nature, 50-52; concern with imperial matters, 20-22; influence on creation of American customs board, 123-130, on extension of writs of assistance to America, 132, on restrictions of colonial coastal shipping, 134-136, on Sugar Act, 110-119, on Townshend Duties, 123-132; permanency of appointments, 7; personal relations with first lords of the treasury, 82-85; position under treasury, 15, 16n, 20-22; report of in 1759, 112-113; share power equally, 51

customs, commissioners of for America, 11, 15, 86, 123, 124, 125, 128, 129, 130, 131, 137, 184; influence of English customs commissioners on creation of, 123-130

customs officers, American, 124

customs, secretary to commissioners of, 87, 171; involved to some extent in politics, 47

Darby, Admiral George, 157

Dartmouth, William Legge, 2nd Earl of, secretary of state to the American department, 9, 139, 140, 141, 142, 143, 144, 167; influenced by John Pow-

nall, 74-76; introduces Quebec Act in House of Lords, 149

DeGrey, William, attorney general, 131

Delancy, James, lieutenant governor of New York, death of, 70

Eden, William (1st Baron Auckland), undersecretary of state, 119, 143, 155; intelligence operations of, 169; political apprenticeship of, 42

Egremont, Charles Wyndham, 2nd Earl of, secretary of state, 116, 182; death of, 93; influence of on Proclamation of 1763, 89-91

Ellis, Henry, governor of Georgia, tries to use William Knox's influence, 13n, 68

Fairfax, Brian, customs commissioner, 51

Fox, Charles James, 159; bill of to regulate trade by orders in council, 178n

Fox-North coalition, American trade measures of, 176-178

Franklin, Benjamin, and the Whately letters, 187-188

Fraser, William, undersecretary of state, correspondence of with John Robinson, 165-166; attempts to improve transportation service, 173-174

Gage, General Thomas, 143, 146; commission of as governor of Massachusetts, 147; opinion of regarding Commissary Campbell, 74

Gare, Francis, attempts to ship gunpowder illegally, 80-82

221

Index

Index

Ingersoll, Jared, 101, 110, 193; views of sought concerning Sugar Act, 102; advises against Stamp Act, 103

Jackson, Richard, legal advisor to the board of trade, 61, 118
Jenkinson, Charles (1st Earl of Liverpool), 59, 101, 104, 106, 114, 115, 119, 156, 177, 181, 185, 192; political apprenticeship of, 42; responsibility of for correspondence as undersecretary of state, 34
Johnson, Sir William, 75

king's friends, 181
Knox, William, undersecretary to the American department, 4, 13n, 68, 139, 140, 143, 146, 149, 150, 151, 152, 175, 177, 178; attempts of to improve communications, 171; attempts of to improve transportation services, 173; career of, 42-44; helped by John Pownall, 74; measures of regarding American trade, 177, 177n, 178; pamphleteering experience of before joining ministry, 151; plan of to maintain order in Massachusetts, 145; political tracts of in favor of Quebec Act and Boston Port Bill, 150-152; use of intelligence by, 169

Laurens, Henry, 123
Lewis, Matthew, deputy secretary at war, acts upon Philip Stephens' orders, 155, 156
Lloyd, Charles, private secretary to George Grenville, 39, 40
Lowndes, Charles, treasury secretary, 53, 124

Maddison, Rev. Mr., 168
Mallet, David, 45
Marriot, James, king's advocate general, 162; requests Grey Cooper to lay plans before Lord North, 161
Martin, Byam, 77n
Martin, Samuel, treasury secretary, 57, 62, 63; views of regarding treasury secretaryship, 77, 77n
McCulloh, Henry, 104, 192, 193; supposed role of in Sugar Act, 112
Merry, Anthony, contracts for supplying the army in North America, 162-163
ministers, tenure of, 6
Molasses Act, 119
Monckton, Robert, governor of New York, 70
Monson, Sir John, 1st Baron, president of board of trade, 24, 24n
Morgann, Maurice, undersecretary of state to southern department, 91, 93, 94, 96, 152, 185; character and views of, 96; role of in Proclamation of 1763, 93-96; work of on Canadian laws, 95, 149n
Morris, Robert Hunter, chief justice of New Jersey, 102
Mulgrave, Constantine John Phipps, 2nd Baron, 158, 159
Murray, General James, governor of Canada, 148
Musgrave, Sir William, commissioner of customs, 52, 119, 120, 121, 123, 125, 126, 133, 133n

Namier, Sir Lewis, 3, 9n, 16,

Index

ment, 33n, 72-73; loses office
as president of board of trade,
1763, 93; plans of for American trade, 175-176
southern department, role of in
Proclamation of 1763, 89-91
Stamp Act, 10-11, 82, 86, 88,
100, 103, 104, 105, 106, 109,
110, 111, 122, 123, 130-131,
138, 139, 141, 150, 182, 184,
190, 191, 193; administrative
confusion surrounding, 190-
193; British stamp commissioners not important in formulation of, 13; influence of
subministers upon, 97-109;
preparation of, 97-110; support of by William Knox, 42
stamp commissioners, 102, 104,
108, 193; negotiate increased
establishment for American
business, 107-108; not important in formulation of Stamp
Act, 13
Stanley, Edward, customs secretary, 24, 24n, 52, 126, 126n,
130, 136n, 167; blunder of in
allowing copper to reach
France, 167; political role of
as clerk of the northern ports,
47, 48; use of intelligence by,
170
Stanley, Sir John, customs commissioner, 51
Stephens, Philip, admiralty secretary, 9, 59, 62-63, 84, 136n,
137, 155n, 156, 157, 158, 159,
160, 163, 164, 173, 184, 185;
attempts to improve communications, 172; concerts measures with Lord Sandwich
against combined French and
Spanish fleets, 157; concerts
opinion with John Pownall

about artillery for Nova Scotia, 163-164; explains naval
policies to Lord Amherst, 156-
157; friendship of with Lord
Sandwich, 67-69; helps prepare parliamentary defense of
Sandwich administration, 158-
159; helps plan relief of Gibraltar, 157-158; orders impressment upon his own authority, 155-157; political affairs of, 47
Stirling, Lord, see Alexander,
William
Stormont, David Murray, Viscount (2nd Earl of Mans-
field), 173
subministers, advice of sought by
ministers, 7; attempts of to
improve communications, 170-
172; blunder of in allowing
copper to reach France, 165-
166; bureaucratic standing of,
3; coordination of activities of
based on intelligence sources,
168-170; cooperative efforts of
1760's by give way to concentration of influence in American department, 139; depu-
ties or chief clerks aid, 33;
discretionary power of in correspondence, 55-60; duties of,
22-38; influence of on policy,
8-12, 85-87, 96; intimacy of
with superiors, 8-9; limited
number of could influence
colonial policy, 3, 22; methods
of correspondence of, 174; motivations of in American policy, 152-153; personal relations
of with superiors, 64-85; place
of in growth of civil service,
179-180; place of in interpretations of American Revolu-

226